Discovering HEAVEN *A Journey*

MARTIN BARON

FOREWORDS BY
CHRIS REED & RICK JOYNER

Discovering Heaven – A Journey
By Martin Baron

First U.S. edition, 2024

MorningStar Ministries, Fort Mill, South Carolina.
Distributed by MorningStar Publications, Inc., a division of MorningStar Fellowship Church 375 Star Light Drive, Fort Mill, South Carolina 29715

www.MorningStarMinistries.org
1-800-542-0278

Translation: Sabine Njock, Tanya Gardiner
Photos: iStockphoto, Martin Baron

Cover and layout design: Esther Eunjoo Jun

ISBN: 978-1-60708-004-6

For a free catalog of MorningStar resources, please call 1-800-542-0278

Endorsements

The present world, with its limited scientific laws, is not big enough for a born-again Christian, any more than a cage is for an eagle. It needs extending, and that extension is into the fourth dimension beyond our three-dimensional world. We ***"walk in the Spirit"*** **(see Galatians 5:25 NKJV).** *God has* ***"made us sit together in heavenly places in Christ Jesus"*** **(see Ephesians 2:6 NKJV).** *This is true fulfillment.*

The prophet Joel said, ***"Your young men shall see visions."*** **(see Joel 2:28 NKJV).** *Their perception changes. A vision is to see as God sees. God's visionaries will see the invisible and reach theunreachable. Holy Spirit vision turns into concrete reality."* —Reinhard Bonnke

This book is a true treasure. The Scriptures declare, ***"Eye has not seen, nor ear heard, nor have entered into the heart of man the things which God has prepared for those who love Him. But God has revealed them to us through His Spirit. For the Spirit searches all things, yes, the deep things of God"*** **(1 Corinthians 2:9-10).**

There are special benefits that those who love God can enjoy in this world. Two of the most precious ones are to be able to see what eye has not seen, and to hear what ear has not heard.

In ***Discovering Heaven****, Martin Baron not only shares his personal experiences in the heavenly realm, but also encourages us to seek first the kingdom of God and His righteousness. He shares how the Holy Spirit also desires to open our eyes to behold the reality of heaven and to open our ears to hear His truth. The kingdom of heaven is within the reach of our hand! When we realize how glorious it truly is, we readily turn away from our sins simply to experience its righteousness, peace, and joy. And when our eyes are opened to see the face of Jesus, we live for the day that we will behold His countenance again!*

As you read ***Discovering Heaven****, your prayer will become,* "***Please, show me Your glory***" **(see Exodus 33:18)**. —Andres Bisonni, evangelist, www.abm.cc

Table of Contents

PART I: INSIGHTS INTO THE SPIRITUAL WORLD

PART II: DISCOVERIES IN THE HEAVENLY DIMENSION

PART III: YOUR PERSONAL DISCOVERY JOURNEY

Foreword by Chris Reed

As children of God, we need to understand our eternal home—heaven. If we have been born again, we are citizens of heaven: **"For our citizenship is in heaven, from which we also eagerly wait for the Savior, the Lord Jesus Christ" (Philippians 3:20).**

Since we belong to the kingdom of heaven, we must know what this means and entails. As citizens, we have rights and responsibilities, access to the blessings, protection, and provisions of heaven, and so much more: **"Blessed be to the God and Father of our Lord Jesus Christ, who has blessed us with every spiritual blessing in the heavenly places in Christ" (Ephesians 1:3).**

Heaven is not some far away place, it surrounds us; we live in it! Martin Baron writes in this book, "Heaven is the spiritual realm which transcends and permeates our natural reality. Heaven is not somewhere 'up there.' It is not a physical place. Heaven is a dimension that is beyond our human comprehension, and that is all around us. It is present right now, encompassing us; it is not far from us in space or time. It is surrounding us, now and here. That is why you can speak to God in prayer. He is there, close to you. Since there is not the notion of geographical distance in the spiritual realm, heaven is not far from us in a geographical sense, but only in a cognitive sense."

I believe this is a good "starter book" about our spiritual identity and position in the Lord. Martin's approach to this powerful topic is gentle and sensitive. It's as if he takes the reader by the hand and sets off with him or her on an unusual journey of discovery.

One important aspect that is well explained in this book is that children of God often have spiritual visions and impressions that are seemingly incoherent. It was the same for Martin. The spiritual impulses and visions he received were like pieces of a jigsaw puzzle that only came together over time to form a bigger picture. However, by carefully writing these down over the years, the puzzle became more complete, and formed an unusual picture that touches hearts in special ways. This book will motivate you to set off on your own journey of discovery into the supernatural dimension.

As followers of the King of kings and Lord of lords in these extraordinary times, it's more important than ever that our spiritual eyes be truly open. Seeing the unseen, hearing the inaudible—tasting, smelling, and touching the supernatural—is something the Lord has prepared for His sons and daughters. Hearing, seeing, and walking with Him should be our normal Christian life. The Bible says, **"You do not have because you do not ask" (see James 4:2)**. So, let's pray for open minds and hearts. This book will change and enrich your life in amazing ways.

We plan to include this book in our student reading list for MorningStar's School of the Prophets. If you read this with a prayerful, open heart, you will receive great blessings and power to change your life.

Foreword by Rick Joyner

Martin is a well-known leader of the prophetic movement in Germany. He has the reputation of a man with great devotion to the Lord and His truth. Through this devotion, he will not compromise the convictions he has stood for at great risk. He is also a man who is light-hearted and full of the joy of the Lord. This strength to stand for truth with the joy of the Lord are characteristics I have found to be common with those who have experienced the heavenly realm.

I first met Martin for lunch recently in our café with his daughter, Anne, who has been my personal assistant for a couple of years. Martin was a delight from the moment we met. Many people are a pleasure to be around, but this was different. I recognized him as having been with the Lord. He had been in heaven with the King.

When Martin told me he had written a book a few years ago about his experiences in heaven and brought me a copy in English, I was excited to read it. In fact, I was shocked at how good it was and could hardly put it down. He begins with sound biblical teaching on the inheritance of every born-again Christian to see the kingdom, God's domain, and to experience it at will.

In my fifty plus years of being a Christian and having known some of the great men and women of God of our time, Martin was only the second person I have known to teach this important truth about our inheritance to experience heaven now. The other one who preached this was Bob Jones.

Bob taught that we are not only called to experience heaven now, but we are also called to be at home in the heavenly realm. Bob practiced this and led as many as he could to experience this. He taught that the heavenly realm would captivate hearts and compel people to seek first His kingdom. Bob's experience transformed many of our students and youth, as well as the most seasoned and mature elders. I saw the messages some received during this experience have great impact and radically change lives, which Bob seemed to do every day.

As basic, clear, and effective as Bob's teachings were on this, I believe Martin Baron's teachings found in this book are even more so. Bob's and Martin's teachings are basically the same, basing everything on the clear teachings of Scripture. However, Martin's teachings are written, and written words tend to go deeper.

Since Christians seeing the kingdom of God is so important, since God's domain is so much more powerful and preeminent, and since every believer beholding this truth and continually living by it is also important, I will be trying to get every believer to read this book. Once they do, I believe those who are not satisfied with just knowing this teaching but also wanting to experience heaven for themselves, will be changed like being born again, again.

I have written books that were bestsellers all over the world in over fifty languages. I'm not that good of a writer or a speaker. So, I know what really draws people to my books is what I have seen and heard in the spiritual realm. This touches the depth and longing of every human being for the spiritual. This happens because we were created to have fellowship with God who is Spirit. We were created from the earthly realm, but we were created to yearn for God, who is Spirit, and become more at home with Him in the heavenly realm than we could ever be in the earthly.

However, just knowing the sound biblical truth that we can experience the heavenly realm is not nearly as important as experiencing it. This is how Elisha could be surrounded by an enemy army and not be at all unsettled, because he saw the heavenly army that was with him greatly outnumbered the earthly army. This was not only Elisha's reality; this is our reality more so!

Christians stand in awe at the Old Testament prophets, yet we are told in the New Testament we have a better covenant with better promises than they (see Hebrews 7:22, 8:6). Jesus said he who is *least* in the kingdom was greater than John the Baptist, who was the greatest born among women (see Matthew 11:11). That means John was the greatest prophet under the old covenant, which included Elijah and Elisha. This is because he who is in the kingdom can see the kingdom, the realm of the Lord, and walk in that truth. So, it is the calling of every Christian to walk in and demonstrate a greater reality than any earthly reality.

We are called to walk on earth but live in another realm and demonstrate the authority of this realm over any condition on earth. Is that not how Jesus lived? Jesus did not come to show us how God lived but how we must live by abiding in Him. If we abide in Him, we will be seated with Him above all rule, authority, and dominion, as we are told in Ephesians 1:3, 18-22:

> **Blessed be the God and Father of our Lord Jesus Christ, who has blessed us with every spiritual blessing in the heavenly places in Christ....**
>
> **I pray that the eyes of your heart may be enlightened, so that you will know what is the hope of His calling, what are the riches of the glory of His inheritance in the saints, and what is the surpassing greatness of His power toward us who believe. These are in accordance with the working of the strength of His might which He brought about in Christ, when He raised Him from the dead and seated Him at His right hand in the heavenly places, far above all rule and authority and power and dominion, and every name that is named, not only in this age but also in the one to come.**

As the apostle wrote, one key to this is having the "eyes of our heart" opened, which is our spiritual eyes, until what we perceive with them becomes more real to us than what we see with our natural eyes. Then we start to live in this greater reality.

I say "we start to live" because it's a maturing process until we become more at home in the spiritual realm than in the natural. As the above quoted verses exhort us, as well as many other New Testament verses, if we have been born again in Christ, this is our calling—to grow up and mature in Him. What we must do now is not just believe but do this. I think Martin's clear biblical teaching on this will help you.

When we begin to see the heavenly realm where God dwells, of which the natural world is only a shadow, we'll be changed by it and see this world differently than those who only see in the natural. Seeing the kingdom first, above all other perceptions, is seeing the Lord's dominion over all, which is transforming. Martin's book will help you by highlighting the clear biblical teachings that call us dwell with Christ where He is now.

PART I

Insights into the Spiritual World

**"We have ...received ...the Spirit who is from God,
that we may understand what God has freely given us.
This is what we speak, not in words taught us
by human wisdom but in words taught
by the Spirit, expressing spiritual truths
in spiritual words"
(1 Corinthians 2:12-13).**

**"But there is a God in heaven who reveals mysteries"
(Daniel 2:28).**

CHAPTER 1

How it All Began

It hasn't been easy for me, over the last few years, to publicize the book about my journey of discovery in heaven. Although I felt the Lord was not just calling, but even pushing me to do so, I had to overcome my own resistance. These visions, these pictures that were granted to me seemed too personal, in some ways too "intimate." It felt unquestionably dangerous to take something that is unusually precious and important to me and share it so publicly, vulnerable to every form of wounding critique, rejection, or commentary.

In the past, I had seen how prophetic impressions and pictures could be "torn to pieces" by other people, so I approached the publication process with considerable respect. Nevertheless, as the months went by, I received a great deal of feedback that made it abundantly clear what blessings lay upon this highly personal book. Many people have been encouraged and refreshed by it—their love for Jesus ignited anew. As an example, this is what Claus Philippin, leader of the German arm of the International Christian Chamber of Commerce, wrote to me: "We want to thank you from the bottom of our hearts for your new book! My wife and I have now read it, and it moved us both deeply. In this time, when everything that can shake is being shaken, it's good to know that these are the labor pains of the kingdom of God here on earth, as it is in heaven. That's why I believe that your book, inspired by the Holy Spirit, has been published at exactly the right time."

A few weeks after completing the manuscript, I experienced a profound vision that took place within the heavenly Jerusalem. Jesus, who was standing next to me, walked right into a crowd of people who were praising Him. As He embraced people, laying His hand on their heads, or caressing their cheeks, gazing on them with an expression full of fondness and joy, a man made his way to me from the crowd. He said, "It is an incredible privilege that you are allowed to see all of this while you are still a mortal man. Most of us knew nothing about the beauty of heaven before we got here. You, however, are allowed to see part of what God has prepared for His children. That's so you can tell people about it. All of heaven watches with bated breath to see what is happening on earth."

I pray that this book will lead you, dear reader, into a more intense, more intimate relationship with our matchless Lord. That's why it was written. The most important message of this book is, God has far more for you than you could ever begin to imagine!

I am struggling to go forward. I feel so miserable, so exhausted, so parched. How long have I been wandering in this desert? I don't know.

So much pain, grief, disappointment!

All I know now is this unbearable, vast, life-threatening, frightful desert; biting wind throwing dust and sand into my face; rubble; dryness.

There is burning heat by day and biting cold by night. My skin is sunburned, my clothes in rags. I am bleeding, and my eyes are ulcerated.

What is the point of all this?
Why not fall down and simply give up?

Everywhere around me are voices. They are full of wickedness, hurt, discouragement. Still, there is this one voice that is calling me, wooing me, guiding me. I have been following it already for a long time. How long? I don't know. But the longer I follow it, the louder all the other voices become. They scream at me, yelling in my ears.

So, why am I following this other voice?
Oh yes, of course! Because this voice knows my name!

CHAPTER 2

Visits in Heaven

A few years ago, this picture marked the beginning of a series of spiritual discoveries, experiences, and insights.[1] When looking back, they wind themselves through my life like a string of pearls in all shapes, sizes, and colors. It took quite some time before I could make out a pattern in this series of events.

Again and again, sometimes unexpectedly and suddenly, sometimes after a long time of waiting or searching, the Lord gave me insights into the reality of heaven which were, most of the time, crystal clear and often totally amazing.

The insights I share in this book were received over a period of ten-plus years. Many years ago, I started seeking after God with a new urgency and developed a deep longing after the Lord. This desire manifested itself, for instance, in repeated prayers pleading with God to allow me to see His face. I felt like the psalmist who wrote, **"As the deer pants for streams of water, so my soul pants for you, O God. My soul thirsts for God, for the living God. When can I go and meet with God?" (Psalm 42:1-2)**

Some of the prayers I have prayed over and over for many years were, "God, I want to see You," "Lord, show me Your glory," "Father, let me see Your face," and others like them. The way God answered these prayers is part of my discovery journey in heaven.

"Look to the Lord and his strength; seek his face always" (Psalm 105:4).

1 The biblical (Greek) word optasia means look, sight, appearance, vision. Optasia describes the process during which a person receives insight into the heavenly realm and experiences an encounter with the spiritual reality.

At different times, I felt that the Lord wanted to reveal something new to me. He asked me each time if I wanted to see something or if He could show me something. When I agreed, I felt transported into a different environment and experienced things that I often found confusing, amazing, and surprising. They challenged my theological understanding and considerably enlarged my horizon.

I always experienced these revelations in such a way that I was right in the middle of what I saw. It was not a sequence of images, like photos, nor like a movie playing in my mind, but each time I found myself being part of the situation, moving around, listening, speaking, and watching. It was far more than just a visual impression. I was able to direct my gaze onto different things, watch them closely, touch them, and ask questions.

My mind, my will, and my emotions were not switched off, nor were my physical senses. I was not separated from my body or in a sleep-like state, like when one is dreaming at night. (By the way, I very rarely remember my dreams.) I was clearly aware of all the things happening around me in the physical world, but at the same time, my spirit was moving in a different realm not accessible to my body. My body kept functioning normally in the physical realm, while my spirit was actively exploring things in the spiritual realm.

It was a little bit like going for long drives in the car. When you are driving a long distance on your own, especially on a highway, you sometimes don't remember long stretches of your journey. Even though you are driving and using all your physical senses to do that, your thoughts are completely elsewhere, as if they were taking you into a different dimension.

When I had these revelations, I did not have any physical symptoms, like trembling or such things. The Lord mostly gave me these insights while I was going for a prayer walk or sitting quietly at home. It also happened sometimes during worship times or times of intimacy with the Lord. Sometimes I woke up suddenly during the night and received an unexpected insight into the heavenly realm. It was very important for me to immediately write down everything I saw and experienced. Therefore, nearly all my insights have been recorded directly after receiving them.

Most of the time, I felt that Jesus was standing directly next to me. Usually, I perceived Him as a "normal" human being, but sometimes also as a glorified figure, similar to how John describes Him in Revelation.[2]

He was with me to show me certain things. I never knew what to expect, and often He explained to me what I was seeing and reminded me of Bible verses confirming what I saw.

The conversations and dialogues I had in the spiritual realm—mostly with Jesus—did not occur with naturally audible words. They happened "Spirit to spirit" in a way and manner that allowed me to perceive the answer of Jesus very clearly and distinctly in my spirit and even with more clarity and assurance than if I had heard it with my natural ears.

Sometimes Jesus would ask me to sit down and write something which He dictated to me word by word. Some of these writings are included in this book.

2 Revelation 1:12-16

CHAPTER 3

Like Pieces of a Jigsaw Puzzle

Many of my spiritual experiences were at first all single, isolated impressions which, as the years went by, became linked together to form a complex big picture, a little bit like assembling a jigsaw puzzle. Each experience was like a disconnected part of a jigsaw puzzle, apparently not related to the other parts. But the more parts I received, the more the picture became complete and isolated pieces began to link up with one another.

I know very well that even today, there are many pieces missing, and this book can only show isolated fragments of the whole picture. Nevertheless, one can start to get a glimpse of the completed picture. The completed picture is breathtakingly different to anything our human imagination could ever perceive. What God has prepared for us is indescribably marvelous. The biggest superlatives are not adequate to even begin to describe it. They seem weak and shallow. That which God has prepared for us is divine.

If you take the time to investigate these things, what you will discover has the power to transform your life.

"To the Lord your God belong the heavens, even the highest heavens, the earth and everything in it" (Deuteronomy 10:14).

(As dictated by the Lord)

Perfection
Absolute, perfected perfection.

No flaw, no fault, no aging, no decay.

My dominion is perfection.
Do you know that the earthly realm is the opposite of perfection?
It is fallen. It has been handed over to death.

Perfection means that nothing is missing, that there is no lack.

In My heavenly Jerusalem there will be no stone missing.

The stones are the people, saved people who I am calling and who are coming to be perfected in My glory.

My Zion is My people, My city, My children, My beloved, My bride.

Believe Me, you have never seen true perfection on this earth, but with Me you will be eternally amazed about perfect perfection.

CHAPTER 4

Where is Heaven?

Before going any further, I would like to clarify how I understand and use the concept of heaven, to avoid potential misunderstandings.[3]

I consider heaven to be the spiritual kingdom of God, the realm in which He reigns alone and unlimited, where everything is focused on Him. God alone is the center of all things, and everything is at His service.

Heaven is where God is.
Where God, the Father—Yahweh—is, there is heaven.
Where God, the Son—Yeshua—is, there is heaven.
Where God, the Holy Spirit—Ruach ha Kodesh—is, there is heaven.

Heaven is the spiritual realm which transcends and permeates our natural reality. Heaven is not somewhere "up there." It is not a physical place. Heaven is a dimension that is beyond our human comprehension, and that is all around us. It is present right now, encompassing us; it is not far from us in space or time. It is really surrounding us, here and now. That is why you can speak to God in prayer. He is there, close to you. Since there is not the notion of geographical distance in the spiritual realm, heaven is not far from us in a geographical sense, but only in a cognitive sense.

3 In the Bible, the Hebrew word *shamajim* and the Greek *ouranos* each describe the visible as well as the invisible heaven. The biblical word *hagion* describes the immediate presence of God and His throne. In Judaism, already in Old Testament times, there were known to be multiple heavenly spaces—*shamajim* is in plural form—which were in later times defined as seven heavens. This number, however, does not correspond with the Bible. Paul only mentions a third heaven in 2 Corinthians 12:2.

"God did this so that men would seek him and perhaps reach out for him and find him, though he is not far from each one of us" (Acts 17:27).

In the Gospel of Matthew, Jesus refers five times to the "kingdom of God" and thirty-two times to the "kingdom of heaven." Both mean the same thing and describe the domain where God rules unconditionally. The kingdom of God is identical to the kingdom of heaven. Where the Bible mentions the kingdom of God, we can equally say kingdom of heaven. It is a spiritual kingdom which is hidden from the natural, earthly man—the flesh. However, the spiritual man may and shall have insights into the spiritual world, into the kingdom of heaven. The Bible exhorts us, **"But seek first his kingdom and his righteousness" (see Matthew 6:33).**

To "seek" means to actively reach out towards something. It is something that we must do. Jesus tells us to seek the kingdom of God—the kingdom of heaven—above all other things.

Just like John the Baptist, Jesus also explains at the beginning of his ministry that the kingdom of heaven has come near.[4] Ever since our Lord died for us, rose from the dead, and sent His Holy Spirit, this kingdom of heaven is no longer just near, but it is now right here among us.

4. Matthew 3:2; 4:17

CHAPTER 5

Born into the Heavenly Reality

When they hear the word "heaven," most Christians immediately think of eternal life with God. They assume that being children of God, we will go to heaven once we die. Heaven is considered the place we go when our body has died. This way of looking at things is basically correct, but it is not complete and hinders us from grasping the fullness of what God has intended for us. After we die, when we leave behind our bodily life—provided we have entertained a living relationship with Jesus as the Lord of our lives—we will enter the domain of God's reign, which is heaven.

Instead of using the word "heaven" for this "eternity with God," I prefer calling it "perfection."[5] It describes the condition after the natural heaven and earth have passed away, after God has judged the world and has thrown Satan into the lake of fire for all eternity, after Jesus has handed over all things to His Father, and after all ungodly powers, including death, have been conquered.[6]

I am convinced that the moment a person is born again, something very real happens in the spiritual world through which he or she becomes a new creation. This new creation is a spiritual, heavenly creation.

"Therefore, if anyone is in Christ, he is a new creation; the old has gone, the new has come!" (2 Corinthians 5:17)

Through this new birth, a Christian is born into the spiritual kingdom of God, into God's reign, which is heaven. He or she has the

5 1 Corinthians 13:10
6 1 Corinthians 15:24-28

citizenship of heaven because he or she has become a citizen of heaven through birth.

"But our citizenship is in heaven. And we eagerly await a Savior from there, the Lord Jesus Christ" (Philippians 3:20).

From the moment he or she is born again, every Christian is in fact part of the reality of heaven. He or she has been born into it and therefore begins as a baby in the heavenly world. Just like a natural baby, he or she is rather clumsy at first. Every baby must learn to discover, understand, and comprehend the natural world that surrounds it. It must learn to orient itself and move about in this reality. At first, it is completely overwhelmed by all the different impressions all around and cannot handle them. Then a process begins of experiencing, learning, and understanding, which results in the child gaining more and more maturity. It learns to move around in the natural world, to recognize things, and to develop a comprehension of how different elements work together.

In the spiritual world, it is exactly the same. A spiritual baby must learn to recognize, to understand, and to grasp the spiritual world that surrounds it. It must learn to orient itself and move around in this reality. This happens through a spiritual learning and ripening process, until the Christian gains more and more spiritual maturity. He or she learns to move around safely in the spiritual world and gains understanding about what this realm has in store for us.

"Until we all reach unity in the faith and in the knowledge of the Son of God and become mature, attaining to the whole measure of the fullness of Christ" (see Ephesians 4:13).

"And to know this love that surpasses knowledge—that you may be filled to the measure of all the fullness of God" (Ephesians 3:19).

Being born again spiritually brings about something completely new. The Holy Spirit takes residence in the person and is now alive in them in a very real way. The Holy Spirit is God—and where God is, there is heaven.

CHAPTER 6

Growing in Understanding

Unfortunately, many Christians don't understand this, and when it comes to living in the spiritual dimension, they stay stuck at the age of a toddler. They don't grow up to attain the true fullness and maturity that God has for them. Their eyes stay focused on the natural, earthly, worldly, and humanly explainable, and they barely develop any understanding for the reality of the spiritual world and their own position therein.

The devil tries with all his might to keep Christians spiritual infants. He fears growth and hates it when followers of Jesus begin to walk in the Spirit. Since the understanding of how the kingdom of God (heaven) operates releases a powerful spiritual dynamic and power, the devil has taken great pains to conceal this, ridicule it, or make it out to be religious nonsense.

It is sad to say that many Christians, due to devilish propaganda, have an image of heaven that shows people playing on harps, sitting on clouds, and singing endless worship songs. Clothed in white nightshirts and with wings, heaven only promises the following: boredom. But this is completely insane! Nothing is further from the truth. Heaven is a place so marvelous that it is beyond imagination. It is absolute ecstasy! Our earthly life seems colorless, unspeakably narrow, and limited compared to what heaven is offering us.

In order to comprehend the difference, imagine what life is like for a baby in the womb. It is alive and grows, but its life is completely limited. It cannot even imagine what life outside the womb is all about. It receives all the nutrition it needs, but the environment is dark and narrow. The baby is not able to imagine colors, forms, smells, or textures even if it tries with all its might. It knows nothing about sunsets, butterflies, gentle spring breezes, or the colors of a forest in the fall. All this is completely hidden, and the baby cannot even conceive of it.

In the same way, the spiritual world is totally beyond our earthly, fleshly reality. In the flesh, we can simply not imagine what God has prepared for us spiritually. It is beyond our limits and all our experiences in this fallen world. But God, who has given us a new birth through His Spirit—by which we have become a new creation and, so to speak, have left our life in the womb—wants us to grow up into a new spiritual life. He wants to reveal to us the glory and the dimension of the spiritual reality, and He wants to do it here and now.

Satan, however, tries with all that is in his power to direct our gaze away from this unimaginably fascinating and fulfilling spiritual life—our home—so that we look only to the petty, natural, and earthly things of this world. He tries to captivate our gaze and keep us tied up with fleshly matters. Again and again, he succeeded to steal from God's people by inciting them to fix their eyes on the earthly and humanly matters and by pushing the spiritual, heavenly elements right to the edge of our awareness.

Oh, how deprived we are if we believe that as Christians we are limited to the human, earthly, physical possibilities and that the kingdom of God is something that awaits us in a faraway future. We get cheated out of so much when biblical affirmations are rationally explained away due to a limited, immature understanding of the Christian life and when we assume these things are not for us or for our time.

"Father, I want those you have given me to be with me where I am, and to see my glory, the glory you have given me" (see John 17:24).

CHAPTER 7

Blind for the Spiritual Reality

Unfortunately, many Christians live like blind people in the spiritual world because our fleshly eyes and earthly knowledge are of no use when it comes to perceiving the spiritual reality. Let's think about this for a moment. Blind people often cannot recognize colors, shades of colors, reflections of light, and many other things, just like a baby in the womb. They may hear about it, but they are not able to see it for themselves. When someone is born blind, he or she cannot even imagine what it is like when someone describes it. It is completely inconceivable for such a person. Still, the blind person lives right in the middle of an environment that is real, true, and undoubtedly there. It surrounds them on all sides; they just can't see it.

This is exactly the way it is with the spiritual reality. However, God did not want His children to be blind. How can we be victorious with the Word of the Spirit when we can't see anything in the spiritual realm? A blind person, even if he or she has the sharpest sword, is easy prey for an adversary who can see. The well-known passage in Ephesians 6:10-17 speaks of our "battle in the heavenly places." We will, therefore, live a life of defeat if our spiritual vision is not opened and unclouded.

When a miracle happens and a blind person receives their sight, they are suddenly able to see all the things that surround them and can recognize them. They now perceive things they only had a vague idea about before, but which were really there all the time.

The good news is that the Holy Spirit wants to open our eyes, so that we can see into the heavenly dimension and move in it; God wants to reveal to us a reality of which we only have a vague idea up to now. Paul wrote to the Corinthians, **"However, as it is written: No eye has seen, no ear has heard, no mind has conceived—what God has prepared for those who love him—but God has revealed it to us by his Spirit. The Spirit searches all things, even the deep things of God" (1 Corinthians 2:9-10).**

Do you remember the story of Elisha when he was about to be captured by an army of the hostile king of Aram?

> **"When the servant of the man of God got up and went out early the next morning, an army with horses and chariots had surrounded the city. 'Oh, my lord, what shall we do?' the servant asked.**
>
> **'Don't be afraid,' the prophet answered. 'Those who are with us are more than those who are with them.'**
>
> **And Elisha prayed, 'O Lord, open his eyes so that he may see.' Then the Lord opened the servant's eyes, and he looked and saw the hills full of horses and chariots of fire all round Elisha" (2 Kings 6:15-17).**

This is a very interesting example of how the spiritual reaches into the natural and how the prophet Elisha was able to see that which was hidden from his more earthly-minded servant. Following the prayer of Elisha, the servant Gehazi had his eyes opened to the reality of the spiritual world that surrounded them. It had been there all the time, but he had been unable to see it. This did not change the actual situation in any way, but suddenly he was able to see what had been hidden from his physical eyes. What changed was his ability to see, and therefore his understanding. Elisha, the spiritually minded man, had an unhindered vision and was able to perceive this battle situation in the spiritual dimension.

A few centuries earlier, a very similar thing happened to the infamous Balaam: **"Then the Lord opened Balaam's eyes, and he saw the angel of the Lord standing in the road with his sword drawn" (Numbers 22:31).**

CHAPTER 8

Seeing the Kingdom of God

In the traditional nocturnal conversation between Jesus and Nicodemus, one of the Jewish top politicians of his time, Jesus states: **"I tell you the truth, no—one can see the kingdom of God unless he is born again" (John 3:3).**

Jesus links the new birth directly with the ability to see the kingdom of God! Without being born again, we do not have the ability to recognize or even perceive the supernatural realm of God's kingdom. This is easy to understand, because without having become a new "spiritual" being, none of us has access to the "spiritual" kingdom of God. It is interesting to note that in turn, all of us who have been born again are able to see the kingdom of God. Each born again Christian has the potential to look into the supernatural realm of the kingdom.

I believe that the word "see" literally means to look—a true ability to look into the heavenly reality. Through our spiritual new birth, we have the right to directly perceive and recognize the spiritual world. This is a spiritual truth that is highly contested, because the enemy fears those followers of Jesus who advance into the spiritual dimension with seeing eyes, instead of trying to build the kingdom of God with earthly means in the natural.

"I have spoken to you of earthly things and you do not believe; how then will you believe if I speak of heavenly things?" (John 3:12)

CHAPTER 9

Eyes Opened

If we are only able to see the natural, then we have not yet attained what God has planned for us. God has much more for us than we can imagine. Through faith, we can secure our spiritual inheritance, possess our spiritual land, and discover the heavenly realm with the enlightened eyes of the inner man. We can all learn to move around in the heavenly world.

In order to do that, we must understand the following: it is for us! It concerns us! It is real! Life in the spiritual reality should be as real and normal for us as life in the natural. If that is not the case, then it is because the eyes of our hearts are not enlightened sufficiently.

"I pray also that the eyes of your heart may be enlightened in order that you may know the hope to which he has called you, the riches of his glorious inheritance in the saints, and his incomparably great power for us who believe" (Ephesians 1:18-19).

God wants to open our eyes, enlighten our inner man, and give us an understanding of life in the spiritual dimension. He wants us to discover our true home, which is heaven.

In this context, I find the word "discover" very interesting. It really describes exactly what this is all about. To "dis-cover" means to uncover something, to take away the cover under which something was hidden. This cover is that which limits you, which veils your vision, and which does not allow you to see spiritually. It is this cover, this veil, that causes spiritual blindness.

In a marvelous passage in 2 Corinthians, Paul writes about the spiritual blindness of the Jews with regards to their understanding of the new covenant: **"But their minds were made dull, for to this day the same veil remains when the old covenant is read. It has not been removed, because only in Christ is it taken away. Even to this day when Moses is read, a veil covers their hearts. But whenever anyone turns to the Lord, the veil is taken away" (2 Corinthians 3:14-16).**

The veil will be removed when the people of Israel will turn to the Lord. This statement is true in a similar way for us as Christians, as well as for every human being. When someone turns to the Lord, He will take away the veil that is covering their heart, even the veil that hinders us, the children of God, to perceive and discover the spiritual reality of heaven. He will open our eyes and give us a clear spiritual vision. In the verses following this passage, Paul writes:

> **"Now the Lord is the Spirit, and where the Spirit of the Lord is, there is freedom. And we all, with unveiled face, beholding the glory of the Lord, are being transformed into the same image from one degree of glory to another. For this comes from the Lord who is the Spirit" (2 Corinthians 3:17-18, ESV).**

Is this true in your life? Do you really behold the glory of the Lord? Can you see it? Do you have a true spiritual revelation about it? Paul is not writing in the future tense. This is about the "here and now," not about "someday in paradise." He is similarly not writing that this concerns only a few spiritual superheroes, but he says, "we all."[7]

With unveiled face, without anything that would hinder our vision, without cover, without veil, we are to behold the glory of the Lord, which means to be able to look into the spiritual realm. Paul says that this in turn will cause us to be transformed and be more and more like Jesus, which is the sincere heart's desire of every true believer. This

7 In Part 3 of this book, entitled "Your Personal Discovery Journey," I will give you some advice on how you can personally progress in this area.

is also what Paul calls freedom—a freedom that delivers us from our earthly, natural limitations and grants us understanding of the spiritual reality.

"For God ... made his light shine in our hearts to give us the light of the knowledge of the glory of God in the face of Christ" (2 Corinthians 4:6).

CHAPTER 10

What Did Jesus Do?

Jesus repeatedly said of Himself that He only did what He saw the Father do. He lived in complete knowledge of the spiritual reality; He understood in the spiritual dimension what the Father wanted to do and then released it into the natural world.[8]

"I am telling you what I have seen in the Father's presence" (see John 8:38).

Our only model for godly lives and actions is none other than Jesus Himself. He came into this fallen world, but He was not shaped or influenced by it. He did not allow the thoughts, ideas, goals, and values of this world to guide or mislead Him, but He only did what His heavenly Father told, showed, and revealed Him to do. This was the only thing that motivated Him and caused Him to act. He even said that He could not do anything out of Himself.

The same is true for us. It is the only way we can build the kingdom of God. We receive, in a very real way, something from God in the spiritual dimension—prepared works—and then we put them into action in the natural world.

"For we are God's workmanship, created in Christ Jesus to do good works, which God prepared in advance for us to do" (Ephesians 2:10).

---

8 For instance, John 5:19, 30; 15:15

CHAPTER 11

Heaven is All Around You

God told me repeatedly, "The heavens are open!" There is no more separation. It is like in the song of the German songwriter Jürgen Werth: "Heaven is not up above; since Jesus came it is here. The boundaries have been shifted; the door is open now." As a child of God, you must draw near to God, you may draw near to God, and you are able to draw near to God. And you can do it here and now!
It is for now, and it is for you.

Heaven is not far from you. It is not unreachable in space or in time, but it is there, closing in all around you. Your whole being is embedded in it. The spiritual world around you is as real as the natural world.

As born again people, we are "citizens of two worlds." We live in both dimensions, spheres, realities, levels, worlds, and realms. We live 100% in the natural, and at the same time 100% in the spiritual. We are people who still live in this natural world but who are, at the same time, not of this world.[9]

God lives in us through his Holy Spirit. We are His dwelling place. And we move in the spiritual dimension, independently of whether we realize it or not, whether we like it or not. We are transferred to the spiritual kingdom of God; we live under His rule and reign.

"He has delivered us from the domain of darkness and transferred us to the kingdom of his beloved Son" (Colossians 1:13, ESV).

---

9 John 17:15-16

Please note that it does not say that He will one day transfer us to this kingdom, but that He has already done it. Where we are is the presence of the kingdom of God. The kingdom of heaven is where the kingdom of God is—in each person who has been born again, who has surrendered his life, in whom the Spirit of God dwells. Each of His children is a citizen of heaven, and this is not only true in a figurative, theological sense, but in a completely real and practical way. Such a person already lives in heaven.

"For through him we both have access to the Father by one Spirit. Consequently, you are no longer foreigners and aliens, but fellow citizens with God's people and members of God's household" (Ephesians 2:18-19).

CHAPTER 12

An Unmistakable Command

The Word of God contains a command that is often overlooked. It tells us, **"Seek the things that are above, where Christ is, seated at the right hand of God" (see Colossians 3:1, ESV).**

God wants us to do what this verse tells us. We should seek the place where Jesus is—on His throne in heaven. To seek is something that is active. We must do it; we must get on with it, get moving. It does not just fall into our lap. Seeking can be something very tiresome, but for those who seek, the Bible promises again and again that they will find.[10]

The very next verse states: **"Set your minds on things that are above, not on things that are on earth" (Colossians 3:2, ESV).**

This statement is even more clear than the first. As Christians, we should not set our minds on that which is on earth. To set your mind on something means to focus your thoughts on it, reflect on it, live it, reach out for it, and desire it. We should not even think about or focus on the things of this world—the earthly, worldly things. I must admit that I do not know one single Christian, including myself, who puts this truly into practice. Are we not all like prisoners of this worldly system? Many Christians think the same way as all the other people around them. They have the same mindset. They have the same preoccupations and fears, and they judge social and political developments in the same way as all the unsaved people around them. But God demands of us, **"Do not conform any longer to the**

10 For instance, Deuteronomy 4:29; Jeremiah 29:13; Matthew 7:7-8; Acts 17:27-28

pattern of this world, but be transformed by the renewing of your mind" (Romans 12:2).

To set our minds on the things that are above means to fix our thoughts on and reach out for the center of all things, the throne of God and the heavenly throne room. Christ is seated at the right hand of the Father on the throne of glory, and that is exactly what we are supposed to seek and set our minds upon. We are not to think like the world around us. The Bible forbids it. Instead, it commands us to seek what is heavenly, divine, and supernatural. So, what is actually preventing us from doing it?

"But we have the mind of Christ" (see 1 Corinthians 2:16).

CHAPTER 13

Walking in the Spirit

We can only perceive the spiritual dimension through faith and only see it with the eyes of our heart. **"We live by faith, not by sight" (2 Corinthians 5:7).**

The Bible calls faith a reality. It is a reality of something that is not visible. Faith is the substance of the heavenly reality. Seeing is according to the flesh; believing is according to the spirit. Faith is not just imagination but the perception of the invisible, spiritual reality.

"Now faith is the reality of what is hoped for, the proof of what is not seen" (Hebrew 11:1, HCSB).

The spiritual world is everlasting; it is eternal; it is the fundamental reality. What we experience in the Spirit is the true reality. We are not just imagining things when we live by faith. It is real! **"If we live in the Spirit, let us also walk in the Spirit" (Galatians 5:25, KJV).**

As born-again people, new creations, and beings that are united with Christ and are temples of the Holy Spirit, God desires that we live in all the fullness of what Jesus has gained for us. He wants to open the eyes of our hearts and give us a revelation of the spiritual world. He wants us to enter the Holy of Holies.

CHAPTER 14

Approaching the Throne of Grace

"Let us then approach the throne of grace with confidence" (see Hebrews 4:16).

In this Scripture, the epistle to the Hebrews speaks about the Holy of Holies. The "throne of grace" describes the covering of the wooden, gold-covered ark of the covenant, covered by two cherubs, which stood in the Holy of Holies of the tabernacle and, later, in the temple. It was called the "mercy seat." It is the place where God was seated on this earth, an earthly image of the heavenly reality. The Holy of Holies was a room where natural light did not penetrate and where the ark of the covenant was kept.

> **"Therefore, brothers, since we have confidence to enter the Most Holy Place by the blood of Jesus, by a new and living way opened for us through the curtain, that is, his body, and since we have a great priest over the house of God, let us draw near to God with a sincere heart in full assurance of faith, having our hearts sprinkled to cleanse us from a guilty conscience and having our bodies washed with pure water" (Hebrews 10:19-22).**

In the days of the old covenant, only one person—the spiritual head of the people, the officiating High Priest—entered the Holy of Holies only once every year on Yom Kippur, the Day of Atonement. With blood, incense, and glowing coals as the only source of natural light, he was allowed to penetrate behind the curtain, enter into the glory of God, the Shekinah[11], and approach the mercy seat. In a most holy ceremony, he offered blood as an atonement offering for the sins of all the people. Yom Kippur celebrates the reconciliation with God. It is the day of entering into the glory of the Lord. On this day, one person was allowed to be face to face with God and to go behind the curtain.

When Jesus died for us on the cross, God tore apart this very curtain. It was completely parted from top to bottom. Suddenly, the Holy of Holies was open, the separation had disappeared. In Jesus' day, this was not just a simple curtain that separated the Holy of Holies from the Holy Place. It was rather an enormous carpet that was several inches thick. It was so heavy that it could only be moved with special rope winches so the high priest could slip behind it. Only God was able to tear it apart.

The fact that 2,000 years ago, the temple curtain was torn in two in the natural from top to bottom—starting from God's side—means, spiritually speaking, that access to the throne of grace is now open. God's children under the new covenant have free access to God. There is no more separation. The path is clear, and we can come directly before the throne of God at any time.

It is important for you to understand that this is not just valid in a theological sense, but that it is real.

The way to the heavenly throne room is free. The veil has been taken away. We can draw near to God with confidence, boldly. We can enter into the realm of the heavenly reality. The doors of heaven are open.

The author of Hebrews unmistakably puts it to us in a nutshell:

"You have not come to a mountain that can be touched ...

11 The word shekinah designates the "indwelling of God" in the natural world. The word is taken from the Hebrew shakan, meaning to put up camp, to settle. Already in Old Testament times, Judaism describes the presence of God on earth in terms of putting up a tent, dwelling, or settling also in relation with the tabernacle and the temple. It is the visible presence of God in space and time, a revelation of his glory in our natural world, normally represented by a glow of light or a radiant cloud, as at the transfiguration of Jesus.

> **But you have come to Mount Zion, to the heavenly Jerusalem, the city of the living God. You have come to thousands upon thousands of angels in joyful assembly, to the church of the firstborn, whose names are written in heaven. You have come to God, the judge of all men, to the spirits of righteous men made perfect, to Jesus the mediator of a new covenant, and to the sprinkled blood that speaks a better word than the blood of Abel" (Hebrews 12:18, 22-24).**

This is what you have come to through your spiritual new birth. This is your home. This is your spiritual life, your inheritance that you can and shall claim. This is the domain of the kingdom of Jesus in which you are to move. You are commanded to approach the throne of grace, the place of the manifest presence of God, right in the center of the heavenly Holy of Holies. In other words, you are allowed to go to the place where God is truly to be found.

CHAPTER 15

Seated in the Heavenly Places

The letter to the Ephesians also gives us insight into the heavenly world. The terms "heaven" or "heavenly places" appear several times. It shows us what Jesus has gained for us. In Him we are blessed with all the resources of heaven. It states, **"Praise be to the God and Father of our Lord Jesus Christ, who has blessed us in the heavenly realms with every spiritual blessing in Christ" (Ephesians 1:3).**

He has prepared the blessings of the heavenly realm for us, so that He can pass them on to this dying world through us, and so that His kingdom—the heavenly kingdom—can spread more and more. It does not say that He has given us earthly and natural blessings in the earthly and natural world. These blessings are in heaven. They are spiritual blessings and they are unspeakably more precious than natural blessings. We must actively receive them, take hold of them, to use them for the glory of God. John the Baptist said: **"A person cannot receive even one thing unless it is given him from heaven" (John 3:27, ESV).**

Remember, you need to understand that this is valid now, and that it is valid for you personally. If you are a born-again Christian, then you are already blessed with every spiritual blessing in the heavenly realms. It is true. It is real. It is there for you! But the receiving must be active. You need to get up and get going to take hold of the blessings of heaven. If, so far, you have not yet seized the opportunity to boldly enter the spiritual realms, let that not be the reason to keep hesitating. Even today, turn to the Holy Spirit and ask Him to take you on your personal discovery journey. For you have already been seated in the heavenly places:

"But ... God, who is rich in mercy, made us alive with Christ even when we were dead in transgressions—it is by grace you have been saved. And God raised us up with Christ and seated us with him in the heavenly realms in Christ Jesus" (Ephesians 2:4-6).

(As dictated by the Lord)

Heaven is My dwelling place; it is Mine. Everything in heaven serves the glory of God, exalts Him, and is focused on Him.

God the Father, God the Son, and God the Holy Spirit are heaven. They are the essence of everything beautiful, desirable, good, enjoyable, precious, important, and eternal.

Heaven is not confined in space, for it is as big as God, without limits. Heaven is the reality that is there. It permeates the earthly creation, but creation cannot see it, perceive it, or understand it. It is the reality that will last for all eternity. Heaven simply is.

People, in whom My Spirit lives, live in the heavenly reality. Many of them do not know it, do not realize it, and do not understand it. Nevertheless, in the Spirit they live in God's reality, and in the flesh, they live in the natural on earth. Each of My children lives in two worlds, and I want that each of My children knows about it and reaches out to be able to see things in the spiritual world.

It is because many of My children focus so much on the natural, their gazes captivated and bound, that they are not able to see what the heavenly reality that surrounds them has in store for them.

But for those who ask Me, I will open their eyes. I will take away the veil, and they will be able to see things that will enrich their lives: rich in wisdom and insight, in power, in blessings, in good things that they can pass on to others.

The kingdom of heaven is near; this is always true where people are in the Spirit, where they see spiritually and act spiritually.

My Spirit dwells in my children to give them revelations about heaven—My reign, their homeland, their home, their true sphere of life—not to make their natural, earthly life more bearable.

Heaven is where I am, where the Father is, where My Spirit is.
Heaven is in every person who has been born again.
Heaven is now!
Now and for all eternity!

Reach out for it to discover what is yours. You are already living in it.

Open the eyes of your heart. Open them and see what I have prepared for you.

I am waiting for you.

CHAPTER 16

The Right Perspective

Despite all the obvious biblical references, some Christians consider it altogether dangerous and questionable to take an interest in the realm of the supernatural and the spiritual world. Without a doubt, many wrong and unbiblical practices and worldviews have invaded our society. Faithful Christians, who do not want to have anything to do with these dubious practices, have rejected this so categorically and radically that they now denounce all supernatural experiences. But God's people must not abandon this area to the enemy, just because it is obvious that he is active there. We must not retreat in fear; that would be a huge sin of omission. We must understand what belongs to us as children of the living God, as kings and priests, what is rightfully ours in Christ, and what our heavenly Father expects of us.

"But you are a chosen people, a royal priesthood, a holy nation, a people belonging to God, that you may declare the praises of him who called you out of darkness into his wonderful light" (1 Peter 2:9).

It is tragic that some Christians don't reach out for the fullness of what God has prepared for them, be it out of fear, out of insecurity, or out of blindness. They fear they could be considered too emotional or not sober enough. However, the most "un-sober" thing we can do as believers is to only trust in our own experience and limited knowledge. Insights into the heavenly dimension and an understanding of the spiritual realities is the best protection against temptation and blindness. It is the best protection against being enchained by the cares of this world and the deception of earthly wealth.

It is of highest importance for us to turn our thoughts towards the heavenly realities—that which is above. Only then we will have the right perspective of this limited and restricted earthly life, the things of this world, the difficulties, problems, sufferings, pains, as well as the joys, victories, and successes. We will have the perspective of eternity.

CHAPTER 17

Fulfilling the Command of Jesus

How else could we, the people of God, impact the people around us with the truth of the gospel, if not by the fact that the spiritual world reaches into the natural world through us, the body of Jesus? Jesus Himself was operating in the supernatural to demonstrate the kingdom of God, and He gave His disciples the command to do likewise. He alone is our model. What pretention to think we could build the kingdom of God without the supernatural manifestations of His work and His power. We will not convince anybody by presenting Christianity as something entirely intellectual, theoretical, and rational, even if we use the most eloquent speech. Paul was very aware of the fact that the kingdom of God is not built upon highly eloquent, powerful, and brilliant sermons.

"My message and my preaching were not with wise and persuasive words, but with a demonstration of the Spirit's power, so that your faith might not rest on men's wisdom, but on God's power" (1 Corinthians 2:4-5).

"For the kingdom of God is not a matter of talk but of power" (1 Corinthians 4:20).

What we need is not eloquent speech, not human wisdom, not convincing words—of that we have more than enough in our western Christian world. What we need is a visible manifestation of the supernatural power of God, this power that makes heaven visible on earth, heals the sick, frees the captives, drives out demons, works signs and miracles, and reaps the end-time harvest. What we need is a very real, genuine, and visible "manifestation of the Spirit and of power." In other words, we need the spiritual reality to invade our natural existence; we need the demonstration of its genuineness and power. We need spiritual authority. We need a tangible revelation of heaven.

In his sermon on the day of Pentecost, the day the church of Jesus Christ was born, Peter said: **"Exalted to the right hand of God, he has received from the Father the promised Holy Spirit and has poured out what you now see and hear" (Acts 2:33).**

The people saw and heard something. With their own eyes and ears, they witnessed an eruption of the spiritual reality in the natural world. If our ministry and work for God do not show visible and audible signs of the spiritual world, then it is not really of any use. If we want to build the kingdom of God, then we need an open heaven, a revelation of the spiritual dimension.

Every person knows deep down inside that there is more than what the natural world has to offer. And in some way or other, every person is going exactly in that direction. Having been made in the image of the Creator, we long to experience God and His workings in a palpable and living way. Therefore, this is not to be rejected, but it is very good. God Himself has put this longing in our hearts.

CHAPTER 18

Rivers of Living Water

Speaking in tongues is something that flows out of the Spirit and becomes concrete in the natural through the human vocal apparatus. In this way, the spiritual world can express itself in the natural world. Both realities are intimately linked to each other in the speaking in unknown tongues.

I believe that it is much easier for Christians who speak in tongues to understand how the spiritual reality of heaven can become visible in our natural environment. It has nothing to do with personal efforts, striving, or willpower. We only trust the Holy Spirit, open up to Him, and allow Him to lead us into that which conforms with the will of God.

"Whoever believes in me, as the Scripture has said, 'Out of his heart will flow rivers of living water.' Now this he said about the Spirit." (see John 7:38-39, ESV).

Note that it says here that the rivers will flow from the body, the belly, the natural part of the person. The spiritual blessings, the rivers of living water, manifest themselves in the natural. Both "realities" are closely interwoven. If we believe according to the Scriptures, then the spiritual reality will reveal itself through our natural bodies. If we believe according to the Scriptures, then God's invisible reign will manifest itself by taking a natural form. Heaven will be visible on earth. The Spirit of God is the power, the river, the might, the light, the dynamic, and the flood that is supposed to reach out from the spiritual dimension into the natural through us.

For a person who believes as the Scriptures say, it should be normal that the Spirit of God flows through his or her life in great measure—like a river, not like a little brook or a trickle—so that the spiritual reality can have an effect in the natural and so things happen that give glory to God because they are truly supernatural.

(As dictated by the Lord)

You wonder whether you have the right to see heaven already now. You think that I will only take you to heaven after you die.

But your eternal life does not begin the moment you die. It begins with the new birth. At that moment already, the old has died and something new has come. You are already a new creation in Me!

My Spirit takes up residence in you and makes of you a temple to the glory of God.

Where can you find God? In the temple! It is His dwelling place.

You are this dwelling place.

Where does heaven touch the earth? In the temple! You are that temple.

You are not a child of this world. You are My child, and you belong to heaven, to the realm where I reign. And in the same way as I saw the Father when I was walking this earth and did what He told Me to do, so I want you to see Me and do what I tell you and what I show you.

I want you to see Me. I want you to know Me, listen to Me, and love Me.

I have been waiting for you for so long.

CHAPTER 19

An Enclave of Heaven

As already mentioned, in the days of the tabernacle and the temple, the Holy of Holies was not accessible. So, why wasn't it? It was part of heaven. We can compare it with a foreign embassy. Inside the embassy, the laws of the country it belongs to apply. It is not submitted to the laws of the country in which it is located, nor does it belong to this particular country. The territory of the embassy is, so to speak, an enclave. Neither the police nor the military or any such bodies of the hosting country have the right to enter.

The tabernacle and the temple were the embassies of heaven, and even more, they were also a small, earthly image of the heavenly reality. Today, however, there is no physical temple. Since Jesus came and lived on this earth, things have completely changed. The New Testament calls us—the body of Jesus—the temple of God.

> **"[You are] built on the foundation of the apostles and prophets, with Christ Jesus himself as the chief cornerstone. In him the whole building is joined together and rises to become a holy temple in the Lord. And in him you too are being built together to become a dwelling in which God lives by his Spirit (Ephesians 2:20-22).**

> **"Don't you know that you yourselves are God's temple and that God's Spirit lives in you? If anyone destroys God's temple, God will destroy him; for God's temple is sacred, and you are that temple" (1 Corinthians 3:16-17).**

For nearly 2,000 years, each born-again Christian has become a temple of God, a "dwelling" of the Holy Spirit, an embassy of heaven, an enclave of the heavenly reality in the midst of a foreign country, which is this world. Even though we live here, our home country, the country we represent, to which we belong and which gives us protection and provision, is heaven.

"We are therefore Christ's ambassadors" (2 Corinthians 5:20).

Can you imagine an ambassador who is not familiar with his or her home country or who does not know how to orient himself or herself in it? Who does not stay in continual contact with the ruler of his or her home country or visits the home country on a regular basis to get specific instructions? Of course not! This is also true for you. If you want to be a worthy ambassador in this world, you must be familiar with your home country, with the ruling laws and the principles that apply there. Therefore, direct your mind toward the spiritual realm, that which is above.

(As dictated by the Lord)

So many times I have called you, invited you to look, to discover, to understand, to perceive the fascinating life of God all around you—the spiritual world full of blessings, power, joy, favor, grace, and all that I want to give to you and to your brothers and sisters.

I have so much more for you.

But the enemy has succeeded in capturing your gaze, and you are completely caught up with the things that are below: earthly things, perishable things, unworthy things.

I want to get hold of your head and tenderly lift it up so that you can look up, toward the light, toward my face, toward that which I have prepared for you.

What are the eyes of your heart focusing on, My child? What do you allow to penetrate in your inner man? What fills your mind, your emotions, your senses?

If they are not eternal things, then they are not worth looking at. They will burden your heart, dampen your spirit, and steal your joy, strength, and victory.

Look at Me, look into My face.
Do you see Me?
I am here; I want to open your eyes.
You can see Me.
You shall see Me.
You must see Me!

My Spirit lives in you, and through Him we are one—you and I, inseparably united for all eternity.

Who told you that you cannot see Me? Who taught you that the natural is more important than the spiritual? Who told you that life only happens in this perishable, earthly world?

You are one with Me, a temple of My Spirit, and where I am, there is heaven. Where My Spirit is, there is heaven. I want to open your eyes so that you can see. Truly see! Let Me open your eyes and take away all the blindness.

I have much more for you than you imagine. So much more!

Allow Me to touch you and reveal your inheritance.

CHAPTER 20

Manifestations of the Heavenly Reality

Each miracle, each healing, and each sign is something that reaches from the spiritual realm (heaven) into the natural realm (the earth). They are supernatural evidence of God's rule that become visible in the natural. They are manifestations in the natural realm that demonstrate the rule and reign of God in the spiritual realm. When Jesus invited Peter to walk on the water[12], He invited him to step out of the natural reality and move in the spiritual reality.

The Bible is full of reports about how heaven had a direct impact on our earthly existence and reality. Just think of all the biblical accounts of appearances of angels out of nowhere,[13] or fire falling from heaven,[14] or all the miracles, healings, visions, and revelations. One of the main themes in the Bible is heaven impacting and penetrating our world.

I would like to mention a few examples:

- The feeding of the 4,000 or 5,000. The modest gift of a boy is received by Jesus in the natural, multiplied in the spiritual dimension, and manifested again in the natural when the disciples distributed the food. No other miracle is reported so many times in the Bible, which explains to us the importance of this event as a perfect example of how the supernatural works. (see Matthew 14:15-21; 15:32-38; Mark 6:35-44; Luke 9:12-17; John 6:5-13.)

12 Matthew 14:25-31

13 Angels are mentioned over 300 times in the Bible.

14 For instance: Leviticus 9:24; 1 Kings 18:38; 2 Kings 1:10-14; 1 Chronicles 21:26; 2 Chronicles 7:1

- The transfiguration of Jesus on the mountain, when He was overshadowed by a visible cloud of God's glory before the eyes of Peter, John, and James (see Matthew 17:1-13; Mark 9:2-7).

- Jesus entering a locked room, after His resurrection, appearing right in the midst of His disciples. He stepped directly out of the invisible spiritual realm into the natural realm (see John 20:19-29; 1 Corinthians 15:5-8).

- The ascension of Jesus into heaven, when He was taken up by a naturally visible cloud to enter the heavenly dimension (see Acts 1:9).

- The naturally visible coming of the Holy Spirit from the open heavens in the form of a dove when Jesus was baptized (see Matthew 3:16).

- The naturally visible coming of the Holy Spirit on the Day of Pentecost in form of tongues of fire on the people gathered in the upper room (see Acts 2:1-4).

- Stephen, who saw heaven open. He saw the glory of God and Jesus standing at the right hand of the Father (see Acts 7:55-56).

- Philip, who was physically transported through the spiritual world, to a different earthly location (see Acts 8:26-40).

- Paul, who was lifted into the third heaven (see 2 Corinthians 12:1-4); who was present in spirit in different places (see 1 Corinthians 5:3-5; Colossians 2:5); whose handkerchiefs could heal the sick and drive out demons (see Acts 19:11-12); to whom Jesus appeared (see Acts 23:11); and who saw angels (see Acts 27:23-24).

- Peter, who was so full of the presence of the Holy Spirit that even his shadow—which simply means his bodily presence—was able to heal the sick (see Acts 5:12-16).

- Ananias, to whom the Lord appeared to give Him a very specific mission (see Acts 9:10-19).

Under the old covenant we also find numerous accounts of how the spiritual reality reveals itself in the natural world. For instance:

- The burning bush (see Exodus 3:4-6).

- Moses went up on the mountain into the presence of God (see Exodus 19:3). We are told again and again how God visibly appeared to Moses (see Exodus 3:4-6; 24:15-18; 33:18-23; 34:5-7) or to a group of people (see Exodus 24:9-11) or even to the whole people (see Exodus 16:10; 19:11; 40:34-35; Leviticus 9:23; Numbers 14:10; 16:19; 17:7; 20:6) and that He spoke to Moses as a man speaks to his friend (see Exodus 33:11).

- The glory of the Lord filling the tabernacle (see Exodus 40:34-35).

- Joshua had the visitation of the commander of the Lord's army, who gave him very precise instructions (see Joshua 5:13-15).

- The glory of the Lord filled Solomon's temple (see 1 Kings 8:10-11).

Here is a short selection of Scripture passages that speak about supernatural encounters—without taking into account dreams:

Abraham (see Genesis 12:7; 17:1; 18:1)
Isaac (see Genesis 26:1-2)
Jacob (see Genesis 32:25-31; 35:9)
Manoah, the father of Samson (see Judges 13:3,9 and 18-22)

Gideon (see Judges 6:12,22)
Solomon (see 1 Kings 3:5; 8:5,10-11; 9:2)
Elijah (see 1 Kings 19:11-13)
Isaiah (see Isaiah 6:1-7)
Jeremiah (see Jeremiah 1:9-13; 24:1-3)
Ezekiel (see Ezekiel 1:1-28; 3:23; 8:2-4; 10:1-22; 11:1; 43:2-6 and others)
Daniel (see Daniel 7:9-14; 10:5-19 and others)
Amos (see Amos 9:1)
Zechariah (see Zechariah 3:1)
Micaiah (see 1 Kings 22:19; 2 Chronicles 18:18)

David had deep personal insight into the glory of God. This is obvious when we read the following and many other passages in Scripture[15]:

"I have set the Lord always before me. Because he is at my right hand, I shall not be shaken" (Psalm 16:8).

"O God, you are my God, earnestly I seek you; ... I have seen you in the sanctuary and beheld your power and your glory" (Psalm 63:1-2).

15 For instance: Psalms 18:7-20; 2 Samuel 22:7-20; Psalms 27:4,8; Psalm 29:3-10; Psalms 63:3

CHAPTER 21

Knowledge in Part

In the second part of this book, I will share about the things that I have seen and experienced in the heavenly dimension. I have tried to describe things and events in normal, everyday language that really are beyond description. Our language is so limited, and some things cannot be described or put into words in an adequate way. Besides, speaking about God's glory and eternal things is always very difficult and inadequate.

What I am sharing flows out of my personal perception and perspective. What I describe are merely individual facets of a mind-blowing heavenly reality. They represent merely one angle, one single point of view. I am very much aware that there are many others. It is just one beam of light among millions that emanate from our Son of righteousness. God has prepared something unimaginable for us, and all our speech, our vision, and our knowledge are nothing more than fragments. They are tiny pieces of a jigsaw puzzle of truly divine dimensions.[16]

My report bears the stamp of my individual personality, with its limitations and restrictions. It comes as seen through my own glasses. I am sure that if somebody else saw the same or similar things, they would probably describe them in a totally different way.

I am a structured and systematic person who likes to investigate spiritual facts and circumstances. I do not contend myself with the opinions of others. I have a very space-oriented perception. In the

16 Much of what has been shown to other people, to whom God gave insights into the heavenly world, was not shown to me, like for instance the Book of Life, Christ as the Lamb or the Lion, the Cloud of Witnesses, the Wedding Banquet, etc.

past I have studied interior design and worked for many years in that profession, and I really like geometry, architecture, proportions, etc. You will certainly notice this when you read my descriptions. Numbers, measures, design, coherence, and order are things that I am as much interested in as structure, materials, or shapes. People who do not have the same way of looking at things and to whom God has given other strengths and abilities will perceive things in a different way.

It is really like Paul said: **"Now we see but a poor reflection as in a mirror; then we shall see face to face. Now I know in part; then I shall know fully, even as I am fully known" (1 Corinthians 13:12).**

Let me illustrate this with a very simplified example, using the geometrical shape of a cylinder. You can look at a cylinder from different angles. Depending on where you stand, you see it as a circle if you look at it from above, or as something completely different, like a rectangle, if you look at it from the side. Both shapes are two-dimensional objects.

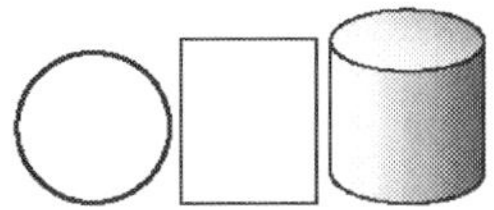

Both angles are correct, but at the same time they are just a limited vision of a three-dimensional, and therefore much more complete, object. Both are "knowledge in part." They are totally different, but nonetheless correct. They are just limited. That is the way it is with our limited understanding of the spiritual reality. What we can see, understand, and describe is just an infinitely small glimpse of a divine complexity that goes beyond anything we could comprehend.

CHAPTER 22

Far Beyond the Human Intellect

"That you ... may have power, together with all the saints, to grasp how wide and long and high and deep is the love of Christ, and to know this love that surpasses knowledge—that you may be filled to the measure of all the fullness of God.

Now to him who is able to do immeasurably more than all we ask or imagine, according to his power that is at work within us, to him be glory in the church and in Christ Jesus throughout all generations, forever and ever! Amen" (Ephesians 3:18-21).

Before going into the second part of this book, and to describe the limitations of our earthly knowledge a little further and help us understand it even better, I would like to take you on an excursion into the subject of dimensions. Hopefully, it will help us in our comprehension of the issue at hand.

As earthly beings, we are merely able to grasp the three spatial dimensions. Some would say that time is an additional dimension, but this is not justifiable, at least from a mathematical point of view. One thing is certain, however; we cannot conceive anything that goes beyond the three spatial dimensions and the factor of time.

Nonetheless, scientists presume that there are other existing dimensions, and mathematicians can easily perform calculations in them—only we cannot understand them because they go beyond our limited intellect. The mathematical or physical definition of the term dimension is very complicated. I would like to explain it in a very simplified way.

A **line** (the x-axis of a coordinate system) is one-dimensional. This line has a starting point and an ending point, therefore 2 vertices and 1 edge.

A **surface** (the x- and y-axes of a coordinate system) is two-dimensional, for example a rectangle. It has 4 vertices, 4 edges, and a surface.

A **space** (the x-, y- and z-axes of a coordinate system) is three-dimensional, for example a cube. It has 8 vertices, 12 edges, 6 surfaces, and a space.

When mathematicians continue this series, it is very easy for them to prove that a four-dimensional "object"—for instance a so-called hypercube—must have 16 vertices, 32 edges, 24 surfaces, and—this is where our comprehension fails us—8 spaces, as well as a four-dimensional hyperspace. This series can be continued indefinitely, and the most outrageous things can be calculated this way. Only, we cannot understand it. Our thinking is simply too limited. God has limited our ability to understand. The reality of heaven, however, is even more complex. It literally blows our minds.

CHAPTER 23

An Excursion into the Two-Dimensional World

Please allow me to take you on an excursion. In our imagination, we will go down to the lower regions of the two-dimensional world. This can be helpful to understand the spiritual dimension.

Imagine a two-dimensional being. It is a being that has a height of zero, whose world only consists in length and width, like a living silhouette. Such a being can neither understand nor conceive the dimension of height, and it never will be able to, because it lives inside a two-dimensional world, where the notion of height does not exist. It simply cannot think beyond this two-dimensional world. In the same way, we as human beings cannot imagine a four-dimensional world.

This flat being happily lives its life. Depending on where it turns, it can look into all directions until something blocks his flat horizon, for instance another flat being. It can move around in this flat world and carry out certain activities. However, this happiness will soon be over when a third dimension comes into play.

Let us imagine a flat surface, like a strip of paper, on which these beings live their life. As soon as you lift the edges of this surface, the horizon of these flat beings changes drastically. It becomes smaller, without apparent reason for them. They cannot comprehend at all what is going on, but the horizon comes closer suddenly, and the beings can only see just a few "steps" ahead.

Someone from the third dimension would be able to draw limits in the life of these flat beings, or could put obstacles in their way, open ways or close them, etc. without the flat beings guessing or comprehending in the least what is going on. He could take hold of one of the flat beings and move them to any place he chooses. Suddenly, it would disappear and reappear out of nowhere in a different location shortly afterwards. Unexpectedly, there could be an obstacle where there was none before. And likewise, a barrier that had been there for a long time could suddenly disappear. Horizons open; horizons disappear. The life of the flat beings is totally unpredictable.

Let us suppose we would take this strip of paper and join both ends to make a ring. For the two-dimensional beings, this would be a completely inexplicable phenomenon. One could go ahead and explore what has happened. He goes off and because of the bend would be quickly out of sight for the others. After having marched for a while, he hears voices and to his great astonishment, meets up again with his friends. Even though he has walked a straight line, he is approaching his friends from the opposite side, from behind. This is inconceivable and inexplicable for a being that only knows two dimensions.

To make the whole thing even more interesting, we will now imagine that we don't join the ends of the strip of paper to form a simple ring, but we will make a so-called Möbius strip. This means that you turn one of the ends before joining it with the other end, linking the inner side of the ring with the outer side. Once again, the flat being will go off to investigate and approach his friends from behind at the end of journey. But once again, something has happened that will completely blow the mind of this being. He reaches them mirror-inverted, upside-down. His bottom is up and his top is below. In order to become normal again, he would have to do the whole journey once more.

You see that a two-dimensional being would be completely inferior to a person living in the third dimension. The three-dimensional person is able to observe, direct, influence, or limit the flat being, without even being recognized or understood. The two-dimensional creature is both completely at his mercy and completely predictable. In the same way, we, as three-dimensional beings, are completely predictable and at the mercy of a being that would be four- or even more than four-dimensional. A four-dimensional being could limit us, direct us, and "twist our horizon." We would be equally transparent and disclosed to him. It could open or close doors for us and step in or out of our existence in the same way.

This thought experiment makes you feel a little nervous, doesn't it? It is an uncomfortable feeling to be exposed and perceived in such a way.

Please don't get me wrong. I am not saying that the spiritual world is four-dimensional. This is not my intention, nor do I believe this myself. The spiritual reality is the "space" where God is , and God is neither limited in time nor space, or in any other way. He is without any dimension. He is God.

Similar to our thought experiment, our lives, our ways, our deeds, and our decisions are completely open and visible to the spiritual dimension. It reminds me of the cloud of witnesses[17] who are around us according to Hebrews, and who are watching us.

This picture can perhaps help us to comprehend the influence and the superiority of the heavenly dimension over our lives. It is not only superior to the natural, but it is completely different, of a completely different nature, something incredibly ingenious. It is heaven!

17 Hebrews 12:1-2

CHAPTER 24

The Door is Open

Jesus left the realm of unlimited divine omnipotence to take up a limited, human, earthly existence. He entered our limited three-dimensionality, lowering Himself in a way to our level. He, the unlimited one, came into the limitations of the fallen creation to reconcile us with God and to show us the way to the fullness of God.

Through Him and through His victory, you have access now to God's world—to heaven. Jesus has opened the door for you.

God has more for you than you could ever imagine!

(As dictated by the Lord)

Martin, the things that you have seen, you have not seen them just for your own benefit. They are things that you must pass on to others. This will cause people to receive a longing after Me and My glory, and they will press into what I have ordained for them. Then waves of glory will be released into the lives of these people.

You have seen the splendor reflected by the facets of heavenly glory. They are only a few facets, and other people will go on to behold other facets. What is important is that they get an understanding about how they can also see and receive.

Heaven has nothing to do with clouds, nothing to do with playing on harps or winged beings fluttering from place to place. Heaven is not how the deceived world caricatures it, mocks it, or reduces it to something trivial. Heaven is something that completely transcends human under-

standing, and whoever mocks it only demonstrates his own foolishness and ignorance.

Heaven is something that has none of the earthly, natural, or carnal limitations. Heaven is the place where I am. The glory of heaven is so unimaginable that a person who goes into it will want to get more and more of it.

A person who loses heaven is like a stillborn child; they lose life itself.

PART II

Discoveries in the Heavenly Dimension

"This is what the Lord says, ... the Lord is his name: 'Call to me and I will answer you and tell you great and unsearchable things you do not know'" (Jeremiah 33:2-3).

"He replied, 'The knowledge of the secrets of the kingdom of heaven has been given to you'" (see Matthew 13:11).

"So we fix our eyes not on what is seen, but on what is unseen. For what is seen is temporary, but what is unseen is eternal" (2 Corinthians 4:18).

CHAPTER 25

A Discovery Journey

During a worship time after a sermon on the topic, "Looking into the open heaven," I caught sight of the eyes of Jesus. He looked at me and told me that from now on He would show Himself to me more clearly and distinctly during times of worship. Each time I would be willing, I would be able to behold Him, and what I would see would gradually become more and more distinct each time. He would show me heaven, the heavenly Zion, the throne room of God, and much more. It would be like a journey of discovery, not unlike a guided tour.

CHAPTER 26

The Land of Promise

My journey started with the vision which I have shared in the first part of this book: I was dragging myself across a seemingly endless desert. It was an unending wilderness of stones, rocks, and sand blown everywhere by the wind, filled with hostile voices full of evil, hurt, and discouragement. There was no shelter, nor any place where I could have hidden. I could only crouch down and try to find some rest in this slumped-down position. But then the voices would only scream at me all the louder. By day it was burning hot, and by night bitter cold.

And it was dark. A depressing twilight was over the whole place. The sky seemed to be leaden and sulfurous. The rocks and stones were black or dark grey. Wherever I looked, I only saw a hopeless, gloomy desert.

I was following a voice that was calling me, beckoning me, encouraging me, and motivating me to carry on walking. It knew my name and directed me through the inhospitable and life-threatening desert, like on an invisible path. As I was following its beckoning, I was moving for a long time in a certain direction, until I discovered on the gloomy horizon a continuous, narrow strip, which appeared to be a little brighter. The threatening wind whipped at me, and every step was a strain. But I knew that I needed to keep walking and that something was there in front of me, which, in my mind, I was already calling "the land of the promise."

I dragged myself forward, and the voice that was calling me became clearer with every step. At the same time, the air around me was filled with voices trying to convince me to give up. As I was moving forward slowly, I realized that the light strip on the horizon was in fact an enormous wall which stretched across the whole endless desert in a perfectly straight line, as far as the eye could reach. The more I was advancing, the clearer I saw how dreadfully high this wall was, and that there was absolutely no way to get through. It was insurmountable.

Next, I must have reached a small, slightly elevated rocky plateau, for suddenly I recognized in the distance, right inside the wall, an area that stood out from the besetting darkness through which I had been walking for so long. The beckoning of the voice came from that exact direction, and so I groped on, fell down as I had already done so often, and scrambled to my feet again. I could not recognize very much, because my eyes were infected and swollen from the sand and the wind. My whole body was hurting, and the voices all around me were screaming in my ears. Soon I realized that the light spot in the wall was in fact a gate. It was an open, inviting gate. I did not know where it was leading, but it was from that direction that this soft voice was calling me—and there was light.

"I cared for you in the desert, in the land of burning heat" (Hosea 13:5).

It took me a long time until I stood before the towering passage, which was leading through this gigantic wall. As far as I could see, the wall stretched endlessly to both sides, insurmountable, like a rampart defying the desolation of the desert. Looking through the gate, I could see blurry colors, bright and shining, and I knew that this would be the passage into a new life.

"I am making a way in the desert" (see Isaiah 43:19).

I stepped into the archway of the gate and was suddenly enveloped by something I would like to describe as a "living peace." The screaming voices ceased, the tearing wind stopped, and I was instead surrounded by fresh air, filled with the fragrance of countless flowers, and the soft murmuring of clear water. It was light. I had the impression I had stepped out of the somber twilight of a prison into the bright light of the midday sun.

This voice that had been calling me for so long I now heard very clearly. It was very close. I stepped out of the archway of the huge passage and realized that I had come into a completely different world. All around me was deep peace. I had come into a Garden of Eden. I cannot describe it otherwise. Even though I was hardly able to see, with my eyes being completely encrusted, clogged, and swollen, I recognized a multitude of colors and countless plants, a bright sky, and a path leading through the fresh, green grass, disappearing behind a soft hill. A gentle breeze was brushing over me.

There on the hill stood the person who had been calling me. It was Jesus. He was waiting for me with outstretched arms. I hurried toward Him limping and fell before Him. There, at His feet, I felt as if His love was embracing me. It flowed through me, flooded through me, and healed me. He kneeled and started to carefully clean my eyes and take away the clogged dirt of the desert. I don't remember what we spoke or if we spoke at all. I don't either remember how long I was there at His feet, but it was like the touch of a healing balm on a painful wound.

I looked around. My eyes were still hurting, but I could see clearly now. Behind us towered the huge wall. It faded into the distant horizon on both sides, but how different things looked from this side of the wall. Beyond, on the other side, was an unbearable, hostile, terrible desert with a biting wind, rubble, dust, and sand. But on this side, I saw a picture of unsurpassed beauty and fullness of life. The land was shining brightly like jewels sparkling with countless shades of color. It reminded me of a well-kept Mediterranean garden full of trees, flowers, fruit, birdsongs, and an air that revives your vitality with every breath you breathe. It was glorious. This is what the Garden of Eden must have been like.

"He will make her deserts like Eden, her wastelands like the garden of the Lord. Joy and gladness will be found in her, thanksgiving and the sound of singing" (see Isaiah 51:3).

I noticed that close to the wall, next to the gate, there was an old wooden cross. It was placed slightly elevated on a small hill directly at the wall, only a few meters from the passageway.

Out from this hill, just underneath the cross, flowed a small spring of crystal clear water. The spring pulsated strongly, and the small brook that the water had formed became a small sparkling, clear river only a few hundred meters further along. At the bottom of the river, you could see each stone shining like a precious stone. I was fascinated by the reflections of light on the quickly rushing river.

Jesus told me to take my clothes off and to step into the water. I was surprised, but I gladly started to take off my completely worn-out clothes. The moment I dropped my dirty, torn clothes on the ground, they disappeared. They were something that did not belong to this country. I stepped into the water over steps made of smooth, clear stones, which I had not noticed before, and shrunk back. The water was incredibly cold and icy. But Jesus told me to go into the river and to lie down in the water. I obeyed, and despite the distinct sensation of coldness, I did not feel any pain.

What followed next is difficult to describe. I was lying in the swirling, glittering water, and it was flowing all over and around me, and then I noticed that it was also flowing through me. It was a sensation that is hardly describable. On the outside, it washed all the dirt of the desert, the pus, and scabs, healed the wounds, and was incredibly refreshing. But something else happened inside of me. I had the feeling as if the cold, clear water was washing away half-rotten flesh in me, cleansing me in that way. It felt like a natural sponge through which water flows, washing away all the remains of organic life, until only the sponge itself remains, completely cleansed. I was able to see my own body, and it looked completely normal, even better than before, because it was entirely healed and invigorated. Nevertheless, from inside of me all remains of dirt, garbage and rotten organic substances were washed away. The water was flowing through me, taking away everything impure.

"Having ... our bodies washed with pure water" (see Hebrews 10:22).

After a while, Jesus stretched out His hand toward me to help me get out of the water. I felt completely purified, totally alive, and simply glorious. Then He put a white garment on me and took me in His arms for the first time. Shortly afterwards, He told me to sit down and write down what He was going to dictate to me.

(As dictated by the Lord)

On this day I was greatly rejoicing. My dear Martin had come, and I could see how he was staggering, calling Me, and trying to see. But his eyes were still full of the sand that the desert had blown in.

He came out of the desert, out the dry, barren, empty land, full of heat, cold, and storms. He was panting for fresh water, hungry for fresh fruit—sweet and juicy, refreshing, invigorating, full of life, full of love.

There he was, coming through the barren land that slowly became greener. And he came straight toward Me, guided by My Spirit. He did not look to the left or to the right, for he was thirsting. For Me. He was longing. For Me. He was craving. For Me. He wanted Me, was fed up with the desert, and wanted fullness. The fullness of God. Not just a little bit, but the full breadth and width, length, and depth. He wanted Me, God!

And he came, thirsty and hungry, hands outstretched because he couldn't see with his eyes. And I called him, beckoned him, and called him by name, for I know that I love him and My heart longs for him, yearns for him, My beloved. I have waited for so long for him, stretched out My hands for such a long time for him, and now he has come. He is here!

He allowed Me to cleanse his eyes and to open them, these eyes that have been closed for so long. Clogged up, encrusted with dirt from the desert. And he opened his eyes. And he recognized Me. And he was amazed. I caressed him and beamed at him, and he just stood there amazed and incredulous at what was happening.

And he caressed My cheek, took My hand, clumsily, feeling the place hardened by the scars. And in disbelief over the fact that his longing had been fulfilled, he closed his eyes and opened them again, and I seized him and took him in My arms—and he allowed himself to embrace Me.

Oh, how I rejoice! He is here. And I say: Come, we will go into the land of your promise. A wonderful land! A walk through a beautiful landscape, toward Him, the goal Himself! A garden full of beauty and glory! Full of silvery rivers, huge mountains, and a sea, full of avenues, full of secrets, full of green woods, meadows and flowers and shady places. A land full of sunshine! Full of closeness and friendliness, yes full of friendliness. Taste and see that the Lord is good. How tender, how affectionate, how merciful! Full of goodness, mercy, and grace! Full of loving affection and care!

Come! We will go into that land. The air will heal your eyes; the fruit will revive you and meet your needs. The beauty of the land will bring joy to your heart, heal your wounds, and strengthen your trust and your love. The way with Me is not stony, narrow, tedious, barren, empty, dangerous, or full of ravines and precipices.

There is just one single door to access it, a huge gate before the endless desert. For those who do not find this door, which is a true love for Me, a true faith in Me, how can they find the land? Many think, with Me, there is only grassland, and they are glad to have come out of the desert into the grassland. They think, this is it! But they never taste what I really have in store for them: streams of living water, true drink, and true food.

The desert is big, the door is small, but the path behind it is glorious, full of joys and mercies. Absolutely beautiful! It has been prepared out of love for those who love Me. Rejoice over Me. Come, give Me your hand, we will go into the land. Walking!

Come!
Obey My pleading.
Take hold of My hand, I will never leave you.
And you will love Me, and love Me, and love Me forever.

CHAPTER 27

An Empty Place

I was lying awake during the night. Suddenly, I realized that Jesus was standing right next to me. He asked if I was prepared to see something. I said, “yes.”

“In that case, I will show you a very beautiful place!”

For a short while I had the impression we were flying through space, then I was surrounded by complete darkness. I could see absolutely nothing, and except for a gentle wind, I could hear absolutely nothing. Somehow, I knew that I was standing on a very wide plain. Slowly it became lighter, as if dawn was breaking; it was like a sunrise clouded by a thick wall of fog. The sky was completely white and there were no shadows, no recognizable cloud structures, just a completely pure whiteness, generating light that was even, dim, diffused, and nonetheless very bright.

First, I thought that I was standing on a high, level plateau in a desert, but everything around me was spotless and white. A white, smooth surface stretched into all directions unto the horizon, as far as the eye could see. This surface was completely even; there were no humps or anything of the kind. Then I thought I was standing on clouds, but I was standing on solid ground. Was it perhaps a plain of ice in the Arctic? Or a huge frozen lake? Or a gigantic saltpan in the desert? I perceived this environment neither as cold nor warm. It was a peculiar place. It was completely empty. No birdsong, no tree, not even one single blade of grass. There was absolutely nothing to see. It was a place where there was literally nothing at all! This place was completely empty. There was only this huge, even, bright, white expanse.

Then the Lord said to me, "This is the place where your sins are kept."

And after a short pause, He continued. "To Me, it is a very beautiful place! I love it. Some people have heaped whole mountains of stones in this place. But this one is empty because of what I have done for you."

I asked, "Where is the sin?" And He replied, "Wiped out. It does no longer exist. There is nothing left that separates us!"

CHAPTER 28

The Wide Field

I noticed that I was standing on a wide, grass-covered, and slightly wavy surface, which seemed to be very high up on a mountain-top. Before me, the grassland continued further uphill. Behind me and at some distance to my right and to my left, it was going softly downhill. The plain was probably about 1 or 2 miles long. I felt the soft grass under my feet.

I looked around. The deep blue sky was cloudless. Very far beneath me was the land into which I had entered through the gate. I was able to see it completely, for hundreds of kilometers. To my left was an endless, huge ocean, and to my right, equally endless, the gigantic desert, studded with rock formations. From my lofty position I could also see the massive wall that separated the desert from the green shiny land, and in the middle of the wall I could see the gateway.

A little further, a few hundred yards toward the top, stood Jesus. The first thing I noticed about Him was His shiny white hair. I ran toward Him. He took me in His arms, hugged me, and after saying a few loving words, He started to teach me a very extensive lesson. In parts, I found very surprising. Here is what He said to me:

In the same way as with the praying in tongues, the ability to see spiritually depends on the fact that you open yourself toward these things in an active and conscious manner. You must start walking, pressing in, reaching out for it, and really seek the face of God. God never just imposes these things on us. Whether we see things spiritually or not is something we must first decide for ourselves. We decide to focus our attention on spiritual things, and to open our eyes, to "lift them up."

"I lift up my eyes to you, to you whose throne is in heaven" (Psalm 123:1).

Jesus told me that in the same way you must open your mouth to pray in tongues, you have to "open" your vision. It does not happen automatically. What is needed is some sort of action which is difficult to describe: a personal readiness and consent to actually do it. You must really decide to get going and fix your gaze on spiritual things.

He gave me the assignment to look at the grass and the landscapes far beneath me, to direct my gaze specifically on certain things. Then He explained to me that this soft, grassy hill was the "Wide Field." On this field, there was going to be only Him and me; it was our meeting place. Here, there would be no enemy and no battles; here, there would be clarity of vision and insight.

"He brought me out into a spacious place; he rescued me because he delighted in me" (Psalm 18:19).

"You have ... set my feet in a spacious place" (Psalm 31:8).

Then Jesus told me to lift my gaze up. After a while, I saw at some distance a peculiar tree that looked more like a bush. The trunk was not compact, but was formed out of many individual thin, branch-like little trunks, assembled in an airy way. This, He said, was the tree of my obedience.

The tree was about 6 to 8 meters (20 to 25 feet) high and bore fruit that reminded me of plums; they were of a purplish blue, with a matte surface. I picked one of the oblong fruits and wiped it off. I looked at the fruit in my hand and noticed that it started to glow from the inside out. Before my eyes, it changed into an oblong, polished, faceted, dark violet, sparkling jewel.

Jesus continued to teach me. All the fruits on the trees on this Wide Field were the fruit of different events in my life. This particular fruit was an act of obedience toward my parents when I was twelve years old. The fruit of the deeds and actions in my life would grow, ripen, and wait here. Each good spiritual act, each deed that was pleasing to God, each prayer of intercession, would produce fruit on the corresponding tree. The trees were planted through our prayers. Each prayer, each worship song, each friendly deed, everything we do that has its origin in the Spirit, would bring forth fruit hundredfold or more. Nothing would ever be lost.

"Bearing fruit in every good work" (see Colossians 1:10).

Jesus showed me that on the side of the hill that was leaning toward the ocean, there were hundreds of very different trees. These trees would produce the fruit of my life. The land beneath me was the land of my life. Here, on this hill, the fruit of everything I did in my life that had value in eternity would ripen. It was my eternal treasure.

"Tell the righteous it will be well with them, for they will enjoy the fruit of their deeds" (Isaiah 3:10).

There were all kinds of trees producing very different kinds of fruit. It all looked extremely neat and park-like, and there was no undergrowth. No branches were lying on the grass, no dead wood, or any fruits or leaves that could have fallen from the trees. It was a pleasure to walk through this grass. I did not notice any birdsong, butterflies, or anything like it. Looking between the trunks of the trees that were planted on the softly slanting hill, I could see the ocean far below, and a part of the green land. I noticed that I was so high up that I could hear no sound of waves breaking on the shore. It was a very beautiful, peaceful view, slightly Mediterranean style, with a joyful, quiet, relaxed atmosphere. The wind was blowing gently, the grass moved, and Jesus was with me.

We reached three huge trees. They looked like enormous sequoia, like gigantic, mammoth trees. I was standing in front of one tree, knowing that its name was "strength." Suddenly, I was lifted about 40 yards off the ground, so I was able to examine its top from up close: a pine-like, sun-drenched bark, clusters of green needles, and cone-like, and tightly closed fruits. I picked one of the very small cones growing right next to the mighty stem. This also was transformed in just a few minutes, this time it turned into a gemstone as bright as a diamond. It was so bright that it was barely visible in my hand, but when light fell on it, it sparkled and shone. It represented a long-forgotten prayer I had prayed for a boy in my neighborhood when I was still at school.

"The fruit of the righteous is a tree of life" (see Proverbs 11:30).

I kept these two gemstones in my hand. Jesus told me that I would harvest the treasure of those trees later with great joy and enthusiasm. These fruits were gemstones, which would be considered so precious on earth that people would be prepared to start a nuclear war to get hold of them.

Then He went on explaining that every person, even if they were not saved, owns such a "garden," where the good fruit of their life grows, where it matures and waits to be harvested. It grows sparsely or abundantly, depending on what and how much the person has sown.

"Those who sow in tears will reap with songs of joy" (Psalm 126:5).

"Your eyes are open to all the ways of men; you reward everyone according to his conduct and as his deeds deserve" (see Jeremiah 32:19).

But then, Jesus taught me that multitudes of people would never be privileged to enjoy the harvest of their riches, enter their inheritance, and collect the harvest. People who have not accepted Him personally and willingly as their Lord and Savior will not even enter the eternal life of God. It is as if these people remain in the wilderness of being lost, and that their harvest, which is great for some, stays out of reach. This will be one of the torments of eternal damnation, to know that there is an inheritance that we have squandered, a harvest that has been wasted and that can never be gathered in eternity.

"Praise be to the God and Father of our Lord Jesus Christ! In his great mercy he has given us new birth into a living hope through the resurrection of Jesus Christ from the dead, and into an inheritance that can never perish, spoil or fad—kept in heaven for you, who through faith are shielded by God's power" (1 Peter 1:3-5).

"You did not choose me, but I chose you and appointed you to go and bear fruit—fruit that will last" (see John 15:16).

There will also be Christians who are saved, but who will enter eternity empty-handed, because they only trusted in their own strength and abilities and had not sown anything of eternal value in this heavenly place. They have not allowed a heavenly reward to grow and mature. Their works were, figuratively speaking, merely of wood, hay, or straw.

"If any man builds on this foundation using gold, silver, costly stones, wood, hay or straw, his work will be shown for what it is, because the Day will bring it to light. It will be revealed with fire, and the fire will test the quality of each man's work (1 Corinthians 3:12-13).

There is enthusiastic and abundant joy in heaven over each saved person who enters the presence of God for all eternity, whether their harvest is big or small. The most important and decisive thing is to have eternal life in God. But some of those who enter have many spiritual treasures that they will bring to their Lord as a joyful offering. Others, in turn, will come with little, and some will even come empty-handed.[18]

18 See also the parable of the talents in Matthew 25:14-30 and Luke 19:11-27

"Even now the reaper draws his wages, even now he harvests the crop for eternal life" (see John 4:36).

"The fruit of righteousness will be peace; the effect of righteousness will be quietness and confidence forever" (Isaiah 32:17).

Sometime later, I was awake in the middle of the night and suddenly realized that I was once again standing on the "Wide Field," next to the mighty sequoias. I touched the rough, heavily furrowed bark, warmed by the sunshine.

I looked around. After a little while I found myself standing right in front of a peculiar green wall. I tried to see more clearly, but there was nothing particular to see. In front of me I only saw leaves and seed pods, quite similar to bean poles. They were intertwined and looked nearly like an ornamental lattice. It took some time, until I was able to recognize that the poles were all positioned around a space of about 5 yards of diameter and that this peculiar plant was something resembling a naturally grown booth.

I knew deep inside of me that this plant was growing roots from the seed in the middle which spread, as if drawn with a compass, evenly around the center point. There, on the radius, grew all sorts of sprouts that intertwined with each other, supported each other, and formed something like green wickerwork. The poles grew up high and leaned toward each other at the top, forming a sort of dome of approximately 4 yards in height. They formed a circular, completely clear space that was surrounded by the shoots that supported and upheld each other. The more the shoots grew and produced leaves, the more the surrounding tent of leaves became compact. It really was a naturally grown booth.

Suddenly I found myself inside this natural space. Through the roof made of living green, I could see the sky, and the sun was painting a fascinating shadow play on the hull of leaves. It was completely still.

Not a leaf was moving, and there was not even a wisp of wind. It was a very peculiar space, conveying a very intense and special sense of safety.

"For in the day of trouble he will keep me safe in his dwelling; he will hide me in the shelter of his tabernacle" (see Psalm 27:5).

CHAPTER 29

The Treasures of Life

Once again Jesus asked me if I wanted to see something. I said, "yes." Straight away He took my hand, and I felt as if we were flying for a while.

Next, I saw us standing in an uninhabited landscape. Directly in front of us was a circular precipice; in fact, it was more like a gigantic, cylinder-shaped hole, with a diameter of several hundred yards and steep walls. It was so big that it could be described like a small valley.

After a while, I recognized things lying on the bottom of the hole or valley. They were precious stones, jewels, silver articles, bars of gold, etc. There were a huge number of objects of value made from precious stones and metals. I recognized many crowns, necklaces, and bracelets made of silver or gold, and many individual gemstones lying around. But all these objects didn't even cover the bottom of the hole completely. It was as if they had been scattered on the ground. I knew that among these objects were crown jewels of unmeasurable value and other things like that, but in this huge hole, they looked more like scattered scraps on the ground.

Jesus explained to me that these were the riches of this world, all the existing precious treasures in this world. This was the treasure of the world. "This is all the world has to offer, nothing more," He said. "For these riches, crimes have been committed, wars have been started, and countless people have given their lives for them and in reality, it is so little!"

Then I saw how suddenly the hole was being filled. Like rain falling gently, precious stones of all imaginable kind, color and shape fell slowly from above into the hole. I could not see where they were coming from, or what was happening to the ones scattered on the ground, but I noticed that the hole was being filled slowly but steadily up to the brim with an unimaginable number of precious stones. They were sinking down very softly, glittering, sparkling, and light being reflected a billion times in the prisms and facets of these costly stones lying there in front of me. At one point, the hole was completely full to the brim. One could not even imagine the bottom of it anymore.

"These are the treasures of your life!" Jesus said. "That is the fruit that will last in eternity; this is your reward! With only two of these gemstones, you would be the richest man on earth."

He explained that in heaven, there will be different rewards for the outcome of each individual person's life on earth. That which we sow during our earthly life, we will reap later in heavenly perfection.

> **"I love those who love me, and those who seek me find me. With me are riches and honor, enduring wealth and prosperity. My fruit is better than fine gold; what I yield surpasses choice silver. I walk in the way of righteousness, along the paths of justice, bestowing wealth on those who love me and making their treasuries full" (Proverbs 8:17-21).**

I had the strong urge to stretch out my hand to take some of these objects in front of me and to examine them. But Jesus told me that this was not yet possible, because I had only produced part of the fruit of my life so far, and that the rest would be manifest during the remainder of my life.

Then, I found myself suddenly right above all these treasures and was able to take a close look at these precious things right in front of me. I was not more than an arm's length away and saw numerous fruit-shaped gemstones. First, I saw one that reminded me of an apple because of its shape, color, and size, and it was glowing from the inside. It was as if it was radiating light from the inside out. It had thousands of facets and was shining in an amazing way. I was able to look right inside of it, even to look right through it, as it was so clear in its red-yellow-golden coloring. Then I saw an oversized pear, emerald green, glittering and shining with thousands of facets. Totally fascinating!

Next, I recognized an object reminding me of a pineapple. At the top, it had green leaves, but these were also cut like gemstones. Underneath the leaves was the actual fruit: a crystal clear, very large diamond with thousands of facets. I knew that it was held together by the leaves on the top through an invisible mechanism on the inside, and that it could be divided into dozens of pieces, like a three-dimensional jigsaw puzzle. It was a masterwork surpassing all human skill.

"Rejoice and be glad, because great is your reward in heaven" (see Matthew 5:12).

One thing became unmistakably clear to me: there will be a reward in heaven! Every person has the possibility here in this life to gather a reward—or as the Bible often calls it, fruit—in heaven. Even the smallest good deed during this earthly life will produce something precious in eternity. And none of it will ever be lost.

"This is to my Father's glory, that you bear much fruit, showing yourselves to be my disciples" (John 15:8).

People here on earth who live in great poverty—it made me think automatically of the Christians in the Far East—still have the opportunity to gather immeasurable riches in the spiritual world.

"But store up for yourselves treasures in heaven ... For where your treasure is, there your heart will be also" (Matthew 6:20-21).

"If any man builds on this foundation using gold, silver, costly stones, wood, hay or straw, his work will be shown for what it is, because the Day will bring it to light. It will be revealed with fire, and the fire will test the quality of each man's work" (1 Corinthians 3:12-13).

CHAPTER 30

The Armor

I noticed that I was once again on the gentle hill, situated high up. I saw Jesus standing on the hilltop and ran toward Him, hugged Him, and laid my head against His chest.

After a while, He suddenly disappeared, and I was once again on my own. Soon afterward, I noticed that an invisible hand was clothing me. It was a very strange experience. I realized that I was being clothed with the different parts of the spiritual armor.

First, I felt that I was clothed with a breastplate, a harness. It was made of a strange, unearthly material and looked more like light. It glowed. It was very lightweight and comfortable; indeed, it was a real pleasure to wear it. It didn't hinder my movements in the slightest, but at the same time I was sure that it would protect me one hundred percent. I looked down at myself and noticed that underneath this breastplate of light, I was wearing a rough, white robe.

Next, I was clothed with a broad belt. I cannot really put it in words, but to wear this belt was an absolute delight. I felt fantastic. From the first moment on, I loved wearing this belt and was moving in full assurance with it.

Afterwards, I received a helmet. I knew that it was decorated at the top with feathers and that its color was copper. It engulfed the head like a hood and was open toward the front. It did not really feel like I was wearing the helmet, but I felt exactly like before, even my vision was not limited by it. It did not hinder me in any way, but it gave me complete protection.

The next thing I received was the sword. It was attached to the belt with a leather strap. The hilt fit me exactly and felt good. The sword was perfectly light, nearly weightless. I made some moves in the air, some turns, and I didn't feel any strain in the wrist; it was as light as a feather. At the same time, it was frighteningly sharp. It was so sharp that I could injure myself with it if I did not pay enough attention. It really was a weapon designed to separate things and cut them apart. One could cut through huge blocks of stone or metal like through butter. It was relatively long and incredibly pointed. The point was very efficient for the battle. When you stung the enemy with the point of the sword, he would flee in pain and panic. The stinging seemed to me even more efficient than the possibility of cutting into pieces with one blow. All this only required a small effort.

I knew that the enemy would never be able to resist this sword. It would cut him into pieces like a spider's web—like a thin, stretched out plastic film which you can cut with a blade.

Next, I received the shield. Again, I didn't notice wearing it, and even when I ran, I could hardly feel it. It was very bright—nearly glowing—and rather big, forming a bright, shining surface.

> **He makes my feet like the feet of a deer; he enables me to stand on the heights. He trains my hands for battle; my arms can bend a bow of bronze. You give me your shield of victory, and your right hand sustains me; you stoop down to make me great. You broaden the path beneath me, so that my ankles do not turn over. I pursued my enemies and overtook them; I did not turn back till they were destroyed (Psalm 18:33-37).**

I then looked down at my legs. I noticed that I was wearing sandals that had a smooth sole and were tied nearly up to my knees. I took some steps to test them, being overly careful because of the smooth sole. I soon realized that I could run very well in them, and that even these sandals were hardly noticeable when I ran.

Then I saw myself from outside my body running down the hill clothed in this shining armor, and into the land lying before me. Jesus was standing on top of the hill. He was beaming.

> **Put on the full armor of God so that you can take your stand against the devil's schemes ...**
>
> **Therefore put on the full armor of God, so that when the day of evil comes, you may be able to stand your ground, and after you have done everything, to stand. Stand firm then, with the belt of truth buckled round your waist, with the breastplate of righteousness in place, and with your feet fitted with the readiness that comes from the gospel of peace. In addition to all this, take up the shield of faith, with which you can extinguish all the flaming arrows of the evil one. Take the helmet of salvation and the sword of the Spirit, which is the word of God (Ephesians 6:11, 13-17).**

CHAPTER 31

The Archway

Once again, I found myself standing high up on the grassy plain. Clearly, without any trouble, I could see the land beneath me that stretched wide, glowing, and sparkling with all sorts of colors. To my left I saw the ocean that stretched apparently limitless until the horizon. To my right was the equally endless desert. In between was the narrow, green, lush, sparkling strip of land that reminded me of jewels of extraordinary beauty. The picture made me think of the land of Israel which also stretches like a long strip of land between the ocean and the desert.

"Your territory will extend from the desert ... to the Great Sea on the west" (Joshua 1:4).

I knew that I was free to move about at ease. I walked around for a little while, and then I looked from above at the great wall separating the lush, green strip of land from the gigantic desert. The desert was more made of stones and rocks than sand and stretched out flat and hostile in a shimmering light. Nevertheless, it seemed dark and menacing. Very far away in front of me, to my right, and far behind me were insurmountably high and broad mountain chains separating the land from the desert. In the middle, between the mountain chains, was the enormous wall stretching for hundreds of miles. It was high and built of massive, oatmeal-colored blocks of stone.

From my position I could see that it was completely undamaged. The separation between the hostile desert and the paradisiacal land was intact and insurmountable. Only in the middle section of the wall, there was this one gigantic gateway. It stood open. There were no doors or anything like it; it was simply an overwhelmingly huge passageway. This gateway was bordered by profiled pilasters of stone that converged in an acute angle at the top. I wanted to take a closer look, and soon I was standing right in front of it. I examined the high rising arch up close. The stones of which the wall was built were ancient, and some were slightly chipped at the edges. I touched them and felt that they were warm with the sun. Small plants and flowers were growing out of some of the cracks. The style of this wall reminded me of the Wailing Wall in Jerusalem.

Only very little sand had been blown into the land through the gateway, which was about 20 yards deep. The picture was very peaceful and generated a warm, comfortable feeling. The wall measured about 100 yards (300 feet) in height or more, and the gateway rose to about 15 yards (50 feet) underneath the top of the wall. The width of the passage was at least 55 yards (160 feet). Hundreds of people would have been able to go through it at the same time.

Through the gate, I looked toward the desert. It was lying still and immovable in front of me. I stepped outside. As soon as I moved my foot outside of the limitations of the wall, I was hit by a lashing sandstorm and an icy wind. I only felt the wind the moment I stepped onto the surface of the desert. As soon as I retreated inside the shelter of the passageway, the desert once again seemed to lie still and lifeless before me. Nothing seemed to happen. Next, I took a few hearty and quick steps into the wind to look at the gate from the outside. I was surprised to see that it was completely painted with blood. Blood that was old and had already turned black.

I quickly stepped back inside and within seconds, I had passed from the lashing sandstorm into the Garden of Eden. Warmth, birdsong, sunshine, and a very gentle summer breeze, as well as the scent of thousands of flowers greeted me from the entrance of the gate. This land was indeed like my Garden of Eden. It was the land that was destined and allotted to me by God, my area of responsibility. In the former times, Adam had to leave his God-given area of responsibility, the

Garden of Eden, because of his sin. Perhaps the gate that was guarded by the cherubs had been like this gate in front of which I was standing now. In any case, Adam had to go out into this terrible desert, with everything he had and was. The fact that I was allowed to enter this land was not something I had earned, but it was because I had accepted Jesus Christ as my personal Savior and Lord. It was His blood that had been put on the frame of the gateway and kept death out.

"When the Lord goes through the land to strike down the Egyptians, he will see the blood on the top and sides of the doorframe and will pass over that doorway, and he will not permit the destroyer to enter your houses and strike you down" (Exodus 12:23).

The Old Testament speaks a lot about the desert. I realized that some of the people of the old covenant had spiritually come, so to speak, from the desert of their lives to this gateway. Perhaps David had spiritually come out of the desert to this gateway and stepped into it, but he was not able to go all the way through it. He saw the land from close by, but at the same time from far away. The peace and the quietness inside this gateway were already sufficient for him. For us under the new covenant, however, the land is open. It stretches in front of us, and we can enter into it—a beautiful land, far stretched and full of breathtaking beauty. It is the land of our lives, lived in communion with the triune God. Because of the perfect sacrifice of Jesus, and His blood shed for us, we have access to all that which God has prepared for us.

CHAPTER 32

An Ascent

One morning, I woke up in my bed with a start. I had not had many spiritual impressions for quite a long period of time, and only a few pictures. I knew that this was my own doing, and that some sort of effort was demanded of me to come anew into that which Jesus wanted to show me. It was not something that happened automatically. I knew that I had to reach out for it and actively seek God and had to start walking on this path, as if ascending a mountain.

I felt that Jesus was waiting for me up there on the Wide Field. I desperately wanted to meet Him. But I was not there.

From a bird's eye perspective, I saw myself climbing a steep, stony face with bare hands. My hands and feet were torn and bloody. I saw how I climbed a last rough, sharp-edged ridge. Behind it, a soft, green field sloped downwards. It was surrounded on three sides by pointed rocks and looked like a nest imbedded between them. Up here, everything seemed much lighter and high-spirited. I took a deep breath of the fresh, clean air. Not very far away from me, I saw Jesus. I ran toward Him and threw myself straight in His arms. I hugged Him, and we whirled around in a circle. I kept on saying, "Jesus, Jesus."

I knew that I was once again with Him. I had obeyed His calling, telling me to "Come up here!"

"After this I looked, and there before me was a door standing open in heaven. And the voice I had first heard speaking to me like a trumpet said, Come up here!" (see Revelation 4:1)

CHAPTER 33

Jesus in Glory

During worship at a service, I was standing once again on the Wide Field. I noticed again that I was standing on very soft, green grass. On the top of the gently ascending hill was a bright light. It emanated from a person, and I knew it was Jesus in His glorified body. He invited me to come to Him, and to my surprise He was calling with a mighty, booming voice, "Come!" Then He called out again several times, and each time it was louder, downright unsettling. I literally shook because of the loudness.

"On the Lord's Day I was in the Spirit, and I heard behind me a loud voice like a trumpet" (Revelation 1:10).

I hurried toward Him. He was glistening bright, totally white. A very intensive, unclouded, white light was coming out from Him. It was like looking directly into the bright midday sun. I was standing before Him, and despite the loud voice, I felt no fear or anxiety. I came to Him as His beloved. He had called me and I was allowed to see Him in His powerful glorified body. That was something I had longed for with all my heart.

"Your eyes will see the king in his beauty and view a land that stretches afar" (Isaiah 33:17).

Now I was standing directly in front of Him. He was clearly much taller than I, and of a glistening, intense white. He was not simply glowing, but the light literally beamed out from Him—an "active" light. I looked at His feet which were clothed with sandals.

In this moment, I noticed something that I would see more often from now on. It was the substance of His body. It was both difficult and fascinating to see and could not be compared with anything known here on earth. It was totally unearthly. His feet were nothing like "flesh and blood" (I noticed that his whole body was like that). His skin that felt like normal skin to the touch seemed to be a crystal clear, transparent shell, through which one could see what was lying beneath. Beneath was a fire-like substance, difficult to describe, which resembled the most "golden, glowing, onward streaming lava." I could see something glowing, pulsating, and moving, something like the glow of a bed of coals or incandescent metal.

Above His feet I saw the dazzlingly white robe. His hands, stretched toward me, were of the same substance as His feet. Despite the beaming and glowing emanating from His skin, I was able to distinguish the scars of the stigmata.

I noticed a golden metal band which embraced the robe like a belt or a sash a little above His waist. Except a narrow line running all around it, the band was without ornaments and its shape followed the ribcage, so that it went slightly upwards at the front, forming a sharp angle. The belt seemed dark against the bright shining robe.

Then I looked Jesus in the face. It really was shining like the sun. The emanation of light from His face was clearly visible. It was like mighty sunbeams. Even though this would have been unbearable for earthly human eyes to see, I was able to gaze upon His face. However, at first I could not distinguish anything except the white shining light. It was like looking directly into the beam of a floodlight.

Slowly, I was able to make out the facial features, the mouth, the nose, and the eyes. The red color of the mouth was overlain by the bright light, but not entirely covered. This was the same for the eyes. I can only describe them like blue diamonds, in fact, it disturbed me that they were so bright blue, blazing with wild, unearthly flames.

I took Jesus by the hands. Even though I had the impression of touching glowing coal or piece of lava, His hands were of a normal temperature, a very pleasant sensation. Then Jesus opened His robe a little, and much to my surprise, He showed me the scar made by the spear in His side. I also touched this scar carefully.

> **"On the Lord's Day I was in the Spirit, and I heard behind me a loud voice like a trumpet....**
>
> **"I turned round to see the voice that was speaking to me. And when I turned I saw ... someone like a son of man, dressed in a robe reaching down to his feet and with a golden sash round his chest. His head and hair were white like wool, as white as snow, and his eyes were like blazing fire. His feet were like bronze glowing in a furnace, and his voice was like the sound of rushing waters.... His face was like the sun shining in all its brilliance" (see Revelation 1:10, 12-16).**

> **"I saw that from what appeared to be his waist up he looked like glowing metal, as if full of fire, and that from there down he looked like fire; and brilliant light surrounded him" (Ezekiel 1:27).**

> **"I looked, and I saw a figure like that of a man. From what appeared to be his waist down he was like fire, and from there up his appearance was as bright as glowing metal" (Ezekiel 8:2).**

CHAPTER 34

A Gaze Full of Love and Power

During a worship time that was very much oriented towards meeting with the Lord, I saw Jesus once again, standing on top of the gently rising hill.

I went to Him and put my hands into His, which were stretched out towards me. Once again, I looked at His transparent skin engulfing this inner glow—like lava, like red-hot metal—and noticed afresh that His hands were of a comfortable temperature.

He was standing in front of me and His whole stature, but especially His face, radiated this extremely bright, even white light. This light was something tangible, like sunbeams that you feel on your skin, as if this light was made of some sort of substance. I was literally bathing in this white, extremely pleasant light. I had the impression the light was passing right through me, and I let it flow through and over me. An interesting detail was that I was able to look straight into this radiating brightness, and that my eyes were not hurting. This would have been impossible on earth.

I saw Jesus' white robe and His golden sash around His chest. He put His arms around me and hugged me close. After a few moments He showed me His right hand, in which He was holding a couple of crystal clear objects that I hardly recognized at first because of the "glow" of His hand. Then I realized that they were polished, totally evenly faceted diamonds, each about the size of a hazelnut. When Jesus turned His gaze toward them, the light emanating from His face fell upon them, and they sparkled with many colors and literally started beaming. There were seven diamonds, and they reminded me very much of the fruit that I had picked from one of the trees here on the "Wide Field."

"In his right hand he held seven stars, and out of his mouth came a sharp double-edged sword. His face was like the sun shining in all its brilliance" (Revelation 1:16).

I knew that these were the seven stars of the seven churches mentioned in the book of Revelation, and that Jesus wanted to tell me something about them. He explained that the seven letters to the churches did not represent the history of the church, something I had always believed so far, but they were rather a picture for the church in its entirety, the whole body of Christ. He told me to read these letters from now on from a positive angle, not looking for the negative points, but looking at that which is really there in the churches because of what God is doing. All parts of the church belong together, in order to form the perfect bride.

I tried to make out Jesus' eyes in this radiant, powerful white light. Suddenly, I could see them for a few moments, clearly and distinctly. I was amazed. There was an expression of power, love, and joy in them. I found great favor and real affection. It was the expression of a truly loving heart. I understood afresh that Jesus loved me totally and entirely, that He desired and accepted me. It was an expression that silenced me—an expression full of love and power.

The following day, I saw Jesus once again, standing in front of me just like the day before. This time I paid more attention to what He was wearing on His head, and I recognized His crown. I noticed with amazement that it was not like the crowns that we know generally. As a matter of fact, it was more like several smooth and simple golden bands, only a few centimeters high and a few millimeters thick, bearing a narrow ridge all around—like the one at the breast belt. There were seven of those bands, each a little smaller than the other, positioned on top of each other. I was surprised by the plainness of the crown, but Jesus reminded me that even the sash around the chest and the white robe were completely plain.

"His eyes are like blazing fire, and on his head are many crowns" (see Revelation 19:12).

CHAPTER 35

Citizens of Two Worlds

Jesus was next to me and was holding my hand. It was night. I knew that we were somewhere on earth. We were surrounded by a natural, earthly darkness.

I heard a person singing in tongues in the dark, and I knew inside that it was a Christian who was in solitary confinement in a totalitarian country. In the natural I could not see anything, only hear his singing.

However, an instant after that I saw the same person standing on a wide pasture, very much like the "Wide Field" in my visions. The person was surrounded by many angels and clothed in a long white robe. Jesus was right next to him and everything was embedded in light, fragrance, and glory. I could still hear the person singing.

I became aware how much we, as children of God, are citizens of two worlds. Our existences on earth and, at the same time, in the heavenly realms always run parallel. It is important that we as Christians understand this and that our vision is open to the spiritual reality. Only then can we put the things that are happening to us in the natural world in the right perspective.

Following this, I saw short episodes of people in the natural who were on their deathbeds, in wheelchairs, in prison, chained in work camps, and similar situations. Directly afterwards I then saw the same people spiritually, in the heavenly realm, occupying positions of glory, just like the prisoner that I first saw.

It is true: as children of God, we are citizens of two worlds—here and now.

"If there is a natural body, there is also a spiritual body" (see 1 Corinthians 15:44).

CHAPTER 36

Further Up

During worship time in a service, I was standing once again very high up on the "Wide Field." To my surprise, however, Jesus was not there this time. I knew inside that He was not there and understood that I would not meet Him again in this environment, which had now become familiar to me.

Suddenly, I was looking at the whole scene from a position even further up. Like an extremely high mountaintop, the "Wide Field" was lying high above the strip of land between the ocean and the desert. I saw the trees on the gently sloping hill towards the west and the north-west. Far below me, I saw the wall with the huge gate. I knew that Jesus was not there, and I was very much confused about it.

But then I understood that He wanted me to climb up even higher. I was supposed to come up higher. This unvoiced summons touched me in a peculiar way. After a moment's hesitation, I began running across the field and jumped up high. Arms outstretched, I literally bolted upwards. I felt as if I was floating at high speed through dark space.

Eventually, Jesus was right by my side. I was not moving any more but was completely still. The atmosphere was very peaceful and gentle, but at the same time solemn and awe-inspiring. After some time, I saw a bright, circle-shaped surface at a certain distance in front of us, detaching itself from the slightly darker background. A little later, I realized that it was a hemispherical object protruding from a surface that appeared vertically in front of us like a wall. I saw that it was shimmering. It was the surface of a pearl standing out from a smooth, totally golden, and huge wall. All around the pearl there was a small, raised rim. As far as I could see, there was only this smooth, wide, golden surface stretching as far as the horizon.

I knew that this was one of the pearly gates of the heavenly Jerusalem. The size of the gate could not be measured, because I didn't know how far away we were from the golden surface.

"And he carried me away in the Spirit to a mountain great and high, and showed me the Holy City, Jerusalem" (see Revelation 21:10).

Jesus said that He would not meet me any more on the "Wide Field." He would show me something new: the heavenly Jerusalem. That was why He would meet me in this place from now on.

CHAPTER 37

The Heavenly Jerusalem

I noticed that I was standing once again in front of the pearly gate. Jesus was very close to me. I contemplated the inwardly glowing, shimmering hemisphere against the golden surface stretching out to all sides and dressing itself as an inconceivably huge wall before us.

Jesus asked me if I wanted to see the city from the inside or from the outside, and I replied, "First, from the outside." Instantly, we were standing very far away and were able to see the whole structure. Before me lay a dazzling, shining, glowing something.

First, I thought that I was seeing the sides of a cube, but Jesus spoke into my thoughts saying that the nature of this city could not be understood by limited human perception. This structure was not a cube as I understood it; it was not even three-dimensional, but rather completely detached from that kind of earthly limitation. This city was heavenly, and anything earthly is not capable to understand that which is perfect. Eternal, heavenly perfection is something we as humans can only imagine, but not fully comprehend or grasp.

I knew that John wrote in the book of Revelation that the height, breadth, and length of the city is equal, as it is with a cube, and it was a figure for perfection.

"The city was laid out like a square, as long as it was wide. He measured the city with the rod and found it to be 12,000 stadia[19] in length, and as wide and high as it is long" (Revelation 21:16).

19 If one applies earthly measures to these dimensions, one can assume that the Greek measure of one stadium corresponds to a length of 600 Greek feet, i.e., 185 meters (or 202 yards). Therefore 12,000 stadia of 185 meters (or 202 yards), equals 2,220,000 meters (or 2,424,000 yards), i.e., 2,220 kilometers (or 1,376 miles). See Luke 24:13; John 6:19; 11:18; Revelation 14:20; 21:16.

The picture in front of me was confusing and not comparable to anything earthly. It was shining, radiating, in part glowing, and consisted of an enormous variety of surfaces, solids, and layers as well as vaulted, spherical surfaces, which were all confusingly nested into each other and penetrating one another. One could liken it to hundreds of different glowing solids and surfaces being projected over and on top of each other by many projectors. Except, this here was real.

Suddenly, we were once again near the golden wall. I could no longer see the confusing diversity of solids and surfaces nested into one another; I only saw the wall in front of us.

It was made of a substance that I would describe as "inwardly glowing gold." I obeyed the invitation to touch the wall but retracted my hand with a fright. The substance I thought was gold was not an earthly substance, nor anything comparable to anything earthly.

"The wall was made of jasper, and the city of pure gold, as pure as glass" (Revelation 21:18).

It was comparable to the fascinating substance I had observed when looking at Jesus' skin. It reminded me of glowing lava, pulsating from the inside, like the glow in the embers of a fire, but rather motionless. This substance, too, was not hot, but felt comfortably cool.

With a start and a fright, I realized something; It was alive! The whole structure, the whole city was a living thing! I was stunned and worried. This gigantic and totally unearthly thing in front of me was a living organism. This revelation did not make me feel comfortable at all. It was not comparable to anything earthly; it was strange.

In the book of Revelation, this object is called a "city," and even I had, without thinking about it, adopted this name. But this did not compare with any city that we might know on earth.

Jesus explained to me that this object was built completely and exclusively with living stones, and that the entire city was filled with life. It was not inanimate matter, but life. God Himself, the Light and the Life, dwelled in this city which was built out of living construction units.

"As you come to him, the living Stone—rejected by men but chosen by God and precious to him—you also, like living stones, are being built into a spiritual house to be a holy priesthood, offering spiritual sacrifices acceptable to God through Jesus Christ. For in Scripture it says: 'See, I lay a stone in Zion, a chosen and precious cornerstone, and the one who trusts in him will never be put to shame'" (1 Peter 2:4-6).

I did, however, not see any individual stones, but only the golden surface that was completely without any joints or gaps, without any flaw whatsoever. The pearly gates shone in a shimmery white amid the glowing gold.

Jesus emphasized that this city—representing the church, the body, the bride—was a picture for something that cannot be grasped by the earthly mind, because of its complexity.

"I saw the Holy City, the New Jerusalem, coming down out of heaven from God, prepared as a bride beautifully dressed for her husband" (Revelation 21:2).

CHAPTER 38

A Living City

I noticed that I was once again standing next to Jesus and could see the heavenly Jerusalem gleaming, shining, and bright at a great distance in front of us.

This time, the main geometrical shape I could distinguish looked more clearly like an interlaced cube. But the object consisted of an uncountable number of glowing planes and curved surfaces, which were partly protruding quite a bit from this inner cube. In the end, there was no recognizable shape, even though the words "cube" and "glowing" fit the best to describe this apparition.

"The Holy City, Jerusalem, coming down out of heaven from God. It shone with the glory of God, and its brilliance was like that of a very precious jewel, like a jasper, clear as crystal" (see Revelation 21:10-11).

Once again, Jesus explained to me that the heavenly Jerusalem is not limited to earthly dimensions, but that it transcends them by far, possessing an unimaginable number of heavenly dimensions. The heavenly Jerusalem is perfect! Perfect in a heavenly sense, a divine sense! This is something completely impossible to grasp in our limited, earthly understanding. As humans, we are capable to think in three dimensions, but in that place, there are no dimensional limits. We will be amazed for all eternity about this divine perfection and order.

I found that this structure could very well be described as a sort of "building" or "construction work," as something that has been constructed, built. In fact, no other designation could describe it better.

Nevertheless, the comparison with a building was at the same time totally insufficient and inappropriate. The whole structure was alive and was literally filled with pulsating life.

"In visions of God he took me to the land of Israel and set me on a very high mountain, on whose south side were some buildings that looked like a city" (Ezekiel 40:2).

In my spirit, I began to understand something. Just like each living creature on earth is made of individual cells, like different parts form a body, or like stones are joined together to form a building, each individual living stone—each child of God—is joined together to form this heavenly creation which Jesus calls His bride. In a certain way, it was completely logical that this city had to be alive. What else is it supposed to be or do in the presence of the almighty God? In the heavenly Jerusalem, there cannot be anything dead because God lives in it; therefore, there cannot be anything but life itself.

I realized that not one stone must be missing, not one. If there was just one faulty or missing stone, this structure would not be perfect anymore.

"Now we know that if the earthly tent we live in is destroyed, we have a building from God, an eternal house in heaven, not built by human hands" (2 Corinthians 5:1).

CHAPTER 39

The Pearly Gate

I discovered that I was standing right in front of the pearly gate and was contemplating it. It seemed to glow from the inside out. The word "glow" seemed to be the only earthly word to describe what I saw. The color, the appearance, and the surface reminded me of mother-of-pearl. The surface was pleasant, silky, and smooth. It shimmered, and I could see far inside of it. The designation "pearly gate" was absolutely fitting.

"The twelve gates were twelve pearls, each gate made of a single pearl. The great street of the city was of pure gold, like transparent glass" (Revelation 21:21).

I knew that the twelve gates were the twelve tribes of Israel, so I asked Jesus to which of the tribes belonged the gate in front of us. To my surprise, I instantly heard the answer: "Zebulun." Somehow, I had not expected this answer. Zebulun was the tenth of Jacob's sons, and the sixth and youngest son of Lea. His name meant "rule" and has also the connotation of "dwelling."[20]

"The city had a huge, high wall with 12 gates. Twelve angels were at the gates, one at each of them. On the gates were written the names of the 12 tribes of Israel" (Revelation 21:12).

I then asked the Lord how far the construction of the city has advanced, because I knew intuitively that the structure was not yet finished. This time, His answer was even more surprising: "Half of the stones that will form the heavenly Jerusalem are still missing. Only very

---

20 Genesis 30:20; Genesis 49:13

few of those people who are still missing already know Me yet or are aware that they are destined to be part of the heavenly bride!"

This made me think that according to the statistics, many of the people that have ever existed are actually alive today due to the population explosion. And many of those people are under twenty years old. This statement of Jesus, that the construction of the heavenly Jerusalem has only reached about half of its final construction size, was confirmed to me inwardly many times during the following months. The full number has not yet been reached.[21]

But I also knew that, for the construction of this heavenly city, the element of earthly time was totally meaningless. This was something eternal, and it did not need another 2,000 years to finish the building. What is needed is the number of living stones fixed by God. And as the number of these stones is growing each day, so the heavenly construction is growing also.

"For here we do not have an enduring city, but we are looking for the city that is to come" (Hebrews 13:14).

21 Romans 11:25

CHAPTER 40

Through the Gate

During a worship time, I saw myself from behind outside of my own body standing in front of the pearly gate. I was only a small shadow in front of the shimmering surface. Now I was able to distinguish how big this gate was. Compared to the size of my body, the gate must have a diameter of much more than 100 yards.

Then, I was once again in my body, and Jesus was standing next to me. I understood that I now had to move through the gate, and shortly afterwards, I found myself inside the pearl. I simply slid into it and was suddenly completely enveloped by this lustrous, shimmering, glowing substance. I was able to freely move around inside this substance, which was all around me, and I could also see a short distance in front of me. It was like an extremely dense, shining fog and reminded me of moving and seeing under water.

Slowly we were moving through the pearly gate. After a while, Jesus stopped. If the pearl had the shape of a sphere, we should soon have reached the other side and stepped out of this substance. However, I could see nothing in front of me except the glowing mother-of-pearl, and, from the corner of my eye, Jesus standing next to me.

Next, I once again saw the situation where Jesus had made me come out of the desert by His beckoning, calling me to come through the high gateway in the mighty wall and enter into the land. I remembered how I had to get into the cold, clear water of the brook, and how this water had run through me and cleansed me. Suddenly, I was conscious of the fact that once again, it was not possible to go any further through the pearly gate without cleansing.

Immediately, Jesus explained to me that He had to cleanse me again. I looked down at myself, probably to check if I was dirty. Somehow, I was expecting that I was wearing a long white robe but was surprised to discover that I was wearing the armor which Jesus had put on me a while ago.

Then, something unexpected happened. Jesus was kneeling directly in front of me and, after a short hesitation, began to untie the tight straps of my leather sandals. He took my shoes off by simply pulling them downwards, without me lifting my feet. Then He started washing my feet. Suddenly, there was water, and without a towel, directly with His hands, He cleansed my feet. Even though I had known the story and the significance of the foot-washing[22] for a long time already, I was very surprised to see it happen in this strange environment. I was moved, confused, and somehow disconcerted. For an instant, I felt tempted to react like Peter and stop Him from doing it; the words were already on the tip of my tongue. But I understood that Jesus was doing something that was absolutely necessary. He cleansed my feet and my lower legs nearly up to my knees. Once He was done, He beamed at me joyfully.

Soon, to my great surprise, we stepped out of the gate into the city. I could see very clearly, distinguishing even far-away objects. I was looking at an amazing sight. Directly beneath us, virtually under our feet, was Zion, the heavenly Jerusalem.

We were standing above the golden city, not very high up, rather as if we were looking down from a skyscraper onto a city stretching out beneath. This sight reminded me of an earthly city, more than what I had seen before. There were structures that looked like streets, buildings, and squares. But even so, the word "city" was misleading. Everything was glowing, pulsating, shining, and very bright. It was so bright and shining that despite the clear view, I was unable to see smaller details. One thing was certain: the whole area before me was busy with construction work. What I saw was an

---

22 John 13:1-17

enormous building site. This city, this living structure, was rising and growing incessantly.

“As we have heard, so have we seen in the city of the Lord Almighty, in the city of our God: God makes her secure forever” (Psalm 48:8).

CHAPTER 41

The City from Afar

I felt that I was commanded inwardly to look. I obeyed, and straight away I stood once more behind the pearly gate, inside the heavenly Jerusalem. Before me was the huge building site of the city. Above me, I saw shining, spherical surfaces and something resembling delicate globe-shaped objects of light.

Suddenly, I was traveling at high speed far from the place where I had been standing, and the shining city became smaller and smaller until it was only like a star shining brightly in the distance. The confusingly nested spherical surfaces and bodies, some of them also looking wave-shaped, were assembling in an overwhelming way all around the city and were altogether visible behind the delicately glowing surface. I saw many light surfaces and geometrical light bodies. They were spherical, vaulted, or flat and surrounded the city, shining their light upon her, but at the same time they were like light beaming out of her. Some of them were only visible as delicate edges; others were like whole surfaces of light, arranged in a complex order that I could not distinguish. I saw something that looked like an enormous house-like structure, also shining delicately. It was hardly visible, but I could make it out as some sort of structure or edifice.

Once again, I heard inside me that this was a dimension that I could not conceive and could imagine only vaguely. I replied that we must be thousands of kilometers away from the city, but the Lord explained to me that earthly measures could not be applied in this place.

Later, I was reflecting about heaven and the heavenly Jerusalem and felt that Jesus was very eager to show me something. I followed

Him, and straight away we were standing in front of the walls of the heavenly Jerusalem, outside of the city. Before me, I saw the corner of a simple geometrical cube or block with three totally smooth, seamless, plane surfaces meeting together at the corner point at a right angle.

I looked up, following one of the outer surfaces with my eyes. It was a faultless, golden surface, stretching out in front of me for hundreds of kilometers. I was marveling at this very precise geometrical figure. But Jesus told me that this cube was the perfect picture of the three dimensions in which we as humans are moving. That was why I was seeing this object, which was beyond any human comprehension, in this way.

He told me to put my hand on one of the golden surfaces. It was completely smooth and still, but nevertheless I felt life pulsating inside of it. I looked at Him and said, "The city is alive!"

"Yes, it is a living being, but it cannot be grasped by human intelligence. It is My bride, full of glory. She is full of pulsating life and beauty. She was worth the greatest bride price ever. For all eternity, I will be united with her. With your eyes, you are merely seeing a geometrical object. But this is not something that was made for your eyes, because they can only see three dimensions."

I knew that only from very close by could I see the city as such a clearly-shaped cube, and that I was looking at one of the cornerstones of the heavenly Jerusalem that the Bible calls precious stones. I asked what it was. Jesus answered, "It is sardonyx."

I saw nothing of the kind, but only the golden surfaces. I could not see any gemstone that was standing out from it or that was visible in any way. The sardonyx is an agate with brown or red and white layers. It is the fifth foundation stone of the heavenly Jerusalem.

"The foundations of the city walls were decorated with every kind of precious stone. The first foundation was jasper, the second sapphire, the third chalcedony, the fourth emerald, the fifth sardonyx, the sixth carnelian, the seventh chrysolite, the eighth beryl, the ninth topaz, the tenth chrysoprase, the eleventh jacinth, and the twelfth amethyst" (Revelation 21:19-20).

CHAPTER 42

The Treasure House

I had a special intercession request on my heart. I heard that Jesus was calling me, "Come!"

Shortly afterwards, we were standing inside of a very large inner room, so large that I thought at first it was a huge cave. It was very bright, and on the walls were numerous galleries. A buzz of activity filled the room.

I asked Jesus what this was, and He answered, "This is the treasure house. Here you can receive blessings. Here I give that which you can pass onto others. You cannot pass on something that you have not first received."

Then He told me to hold out my hands. I held out my hands like a cup, and He put a small wooden box in my hands that an angel had given Him just moments before. It was dark brown, and when I opened it, I found an extremely delicate mechanism. It reminded me of an expertly crafted watch or a complicated compass. The mechanism was made of gold. I was perplexed.

When I asked what it was, Jesus said, "This is a treasure." He explained to me that I had to release it and pass it on. This is what I did by proclaiming it by faith, and without me noticing, it left my hands.

"That's it!" said Jesus. "You receive and you give. I am the Giver—and you only pass it on."

"For everyone who asks receives" (see Matthew 7:8).

CHAPTER 43

A Great Treasure

During a time of prayer for people who are close to my heart, the Lord taught me more about the receiving of heavenly blessings. He explained that I had been praying and proclaiming, but not taking. I was supposed to actively take possession of that which I was asking for—grasping and receiving it—to really get it. I was only able to give to others what I had previously obtained.

Shortly afterwards, I saw myself once again with Jesus as we entered the huge room. This treasure house was an overwhelmingly big hall, bright and so deep that the back part was disappearing in the glistening light, like in a bright fog. The end of the room was not visible. All around the walls were various galleries filled with wardrobes, shelves, and cabinets full of innumerable things that I could not distinguish in detail.

Then, Jesus received something from an angel. He was holding both of His hands together and stretched them out toward me. He was holding a small parchment. It was square shaped, about 3 inches long and wide. I examined it and read:

"You can trust Me because I gave everything for you. I gave you more than you have given for yourself. You can trust My love, My guidance, My power, My direction, My life. You can trust Me. I will never disappoint you." —Jesus.

I knew that this encouragement was destined to the person for whom I had just prayed, and I asked, "What is this?" Jesus' answer surprised me. "This is a great treasure. It has been written with My life-blood."

I held out my hands once again like a cup, and He put the parchment into them. Then I prayed, and the paper disappeared from my hands.

Jesus showed me very clearly that I could not take or use the things in this treasure house as I wished. He alone would give them to me, and I was to share them with others. I would be like a postman delivering letters full of blessings. They were not destined for me. "You are reaching into the spiritual and are bringing them into the natural. You see in the spiritual world with the eyes of faith, and what you see and receive there, that you can release."

We were standing next to each other in this heavenly storehouse, and He said, "There are treasures here for which the world would go to war; there are riches and blessings. They are answers to prayer. All these things must be released. All these riches I want to give to people: healings, restorations, blessings of all imaginable kinds."

Jesus told me that there were, all in all, seven galleries running all around the room. He said that millions of gifts were kept here. The floor, which I had not noticed so far, was of polished stone and was shining. I was barefoot, but my feet didn't feel any coldness on the smooth stone. It was pleasant.

On several occasions, I was able to contemplate this impressive room again and again. When I presented a request in intercession for another person to Jesus, an angel would appear soon afterwards and give Him something, which He then put into my open hands. There were many different things, and sometimes it took me a while until I understood what they were. Here are some of the things which Jesus gave me:

- A big drop of a velvety warm liquid, which filled both of my hands. It was golden, like shining oil, and it reminded me of a liquid floating in weightlessness, forming a spherical "whole," even though it is liquid. This was refreshment, anointing, and equipment.

- A heavy, short cylinder that reminded me of a roll. It was a golden-colored, short telescope. It served to see spiritual things more in detail and more specifically, things that were far away and hidden to others.

- A "handful of glory." This was a small, glowing cloud, radiating light from the inside, made of a soft, supernatural substance.

- A small sword, like a short sword or a dagger. It had a very unusual appearance, was made of one piece, and had no shaft. The handle and the blade were all one. It was extremely sharp and was to be used for close spiritual combat. I realized that if God allows the enemy to come very close to this person, then it is to be slain with this sword.

- A sparkling, completely clear, big diamond—not white but of a deep, blood-red color.

- A "whirl." At first, I could not recognize what it was, because it looked very unreal. It fit into both of my hands, was swirling quickly, gleamed, and sparkled. Sparks were flying out of it, reminding me of a sparkler candle. It would whirl up things which were covered in a layer of dust several centimeters thick. It would bring certain things to the light and reveal what was hidden.

"How much more will your Father in heaven give good gifts to those who ask him!" (see Matthew 7:11)

CHAPTER 44

The Throne Room

I noticed that I was floating inside a sphere-shaped room. This room was very bright and immensely huge, far beyond anything one can imagine in terms of an earthly structure. It was simply overwhelming. The diameter of this room could have very well been much more than 100 miles; however, it seemed totally inadequate to apply earthly measures in this context. Golden light was being reflected from the entire vault, the shell of this room—indeed it glowed in a pleasant, gold-colored light.

In the center of the room was a massive, bulky object made of a brownish, blunt material. I supposed that it was a stone-like material. It was like a huge disc, a flat cylinder, a bit like a millstone, bearing another disc at the top and at the bottom, of a much smaller dimension. The object reminded me at first of a round park bench around a tree, only that at the bottom, there was another bench, so to speak, mirror inverted. It was like a round bench with a circular seat surface both on top and at the bottom. It took me quite some time to understand that this must be the throne of God.

What surprised me was that this throne was oriented in two directions. It was a twin throne with two seats which were not next to but facing each other. Since the throne was floating freely in the middle of this spherical room, there was no top or bottom.

I noticed with amazement that both seat surfaces of the throne were circular. A human being sitting on this throne, could have only looked in one direction at the time, but inside of me I knew that this is not so for God. He is completely different to what we can imagine with our limited and fallen minds. The throne, with these round seat surfaces, was exactly right for him. I knew that he was able to sit on the whole surface and look into all directions at once; indeed, anything less would have meant a limitation of his nature.

"The Lord is in his holy temple; the Lord's throne is in heaven" (see Psalm 11:4, ESV).

It seemed clear to me that one side of the throne was for the Father, and the other for the Son, and that they would sit on the throne in complete unity. Up to that moment, I had always imagined the throne of God like an earthly throne, with a back and armrests. I was also stunned by the spherical throne room with its filigree shell, but the monumental stone was totally contradictory to everything I had imagined before. Even the blunt surface did not fit at all the atmosphere of this room. I noticed that its dimensions were huge—the middle part, between the two seat surfaces, must have measured several miles by human standards.

What confused me was that I didn't see anybody sitting on the throne. This had not been revealed to me yet.

In the immense space between the throne and the outer shell, I saw big crowds of people here and there, floating in mid-air. This picture is difficult to describe. The people in those groups were standing perfectly ordered in rank and file as if arranged according to an invisible grid. The distance between the people was relatively large, in my appreciation about 8 yards. The whole looked like a perfectly regular and invisible network, with people standing at every intersection.

All the people were looking toward the center, toward the throne. Each side of every one of these networks consisted of several thousands of people, so that there were millions of people together in each cluster. Before the bulkiness of the throne and the size of the room, the people were not recognizable individually, and each of the networks seemed somehow transparent, downright delicate, a bit like a mosquito swarm against the summer sky. When looked at a certain distance from above, these networks were hardly perceptible against the bright, golden-shimmering background.

A few times, I passed above some of these clusters of people. Looking at them from a flat angle a short distance above their heads, it was like looking across a huge mass of people. As far as the eye could see, there was an ocean of heads. I realized that the biblical term "army" was much more appropriate than "network" to describe these huge groups.

> **"The Lord has established his throne in heaven, and his kingdom rules over all. Praise the Lord, you his angels, you mighty ones who do his bidding, who obey his word. Praise the Lord, all his heavenly hosts, you his servants who do his will. Praise the Lord, all his works everywhere in his dominion. Praise the Lord, O my soul" (Psalm 103:19-22).**

Deep inside, I knew that these hosts were not just made up of humans, but also of angels standing before the throne in perfect discipline and order. Our God is the "Lord of hosts." I did, however, not see any angels yet.

Something else I had noticed right from the start was a bright, white-golden beam coming out of the middle of the throne at the top and at the bottom. It was like an axis going through the central point of this throne made of circular discs. The beam went out in both directions, until it reached the edge of the outer shell.

Obviously, this bright beam was like an axis, giving some sort of orientation inside this spherical room, so that everything else could be located spatially. I saw that at both ends of the beam, where it touched the shell, it radiated, or rather flowed through it. However, I was not able to see where it went from there.

As I looked at the beam more closely, I realized that it consisted of the same indescribable substance which I had seen in the glorified appearance of Jesus. It was like glowing lava but moving very quickly. Inside, it pulsated, even blazed literally. It was like a mixture of light, water, wind, and fire and was of a physical, tangible substance. "Stream" would perhaps be a better word to describe it than "beam." This glowing stream flowed powerfully and at great speed in both directions—so to speak towards the top and the bottom—from the throne. I did not see any other openings in the outer shell, except these two circular areas where the stream was flowing out of the room.

The stream did not flow in a bed, a trench, or any other form of container, but flowed freely in space, circular, like a jet of water coming out of a huge fire hose or like the focused beam of a search light.

Looking more closely at this stream, it reminded me of the glorious cloud of light at the Old Testament time when the people of Israel were wandering in the wilderness. It had to be a similar substance. Only here, in the throne room, it flowed powerfully, in all its might.

> **"As I looked, thrones were set in place, and the Ancient of Days took his seat. His clothing was as white as snow; the hair of his head was white like wool. His throne was flaming with fire, and its wheels were all ablaze. A river of fire was flowing, coming out from before him. Thousands upon thousands attended him; ten thousand times ten thousand stood before him. The court was seated, and the books were opened" (Daniel 7:9-10).**

I realized that what I saw was the Holy Ghost. He flowed out of the throne of God, the throne of the Father and the Son, in two opposite directions. He had His origin in the center of the throne and flowed in direct line toward the two vertices where it left the spherical room. A voice next to me confirmed that this was the Holy Spirit. The fact that Jesus was standing next to me had so far only been an unconscious knowledge; I had not really noticed it. I was not surprised to hear His voice, but I was so captivated by what I saw that I neither turned towards Him nor continued to talk to Him.

The stream coming out of the throne in two directions confused me, as these were in fact two streams flowing in different directions. I was very surprised to see it flowing simultaneously in two directions, for I had always assumed that He would flow out from the throne like a normal river.

I looked at the upper surface of one of the armrests of the throne. It was completely even and formed a big, circular surface. In the middle was something like a crater, a very large hole occupying more or less half of the diameter. I saw that there were trees growing all around this hole. There were thousands.

"Then the angel showed me the river of the water of life ... on each side of the river stood the tree of life" (see Revelation 22:1-2).

"And by the river upon the bank thereof, on this side and on that side, shall grow all trees ... their waters they issued out of the sanctuary" (see Ezekiel 47:12).

This stream coming forth in two directions was much more powerful and fascinating than an earthly river. It was the brightest thing visible in the room and glowed clearly brighter and whiter than the golden-shining shell. On top of that, it was the only thing in the whole throne room that was actually moving.

All around the throne, but still in quite some distance away were several white objects floating freely in the room at the height of the middle disc. I came closer and distinguished that they were white, chair-like objects which would have been considered large according to human thinking. I saw that they were not empty, but that people were sitting on them. (I understood that they were the thrones of the twenty-four ancient ones.) These thrones were arranged perpendicularly to the seat surfaces of the big throne. Their seat surfaces were at a right angle to both seat surfaces of the big throne. If a person sitting on one of those thrones would stretch out his arms to both sides, they would point in both directions of the stream of the Holy Spirit. One arm would be pointing to the throne of the Father, the other to the one of the Son. The twenty-four were arranged at equal distance, just like on a pearl string, all around the divine throne.

After a short while, my position changed, and I found myself far up above, literally at the zenith of the sphere-shaped room. I saw at mid-height, around the throne, and pointing in all four "cardinal" directions, four incredibly large, oblong objects, reminding me of huge tubes. I knew that these objects were living creatures. They appeared, from my viewpoint far up above, as bright and golden as the outer shell, and they were by far the scariest thing that I had observed in this huge, mind-blowing room. Just because of their sizes and the totally unearthly shape, they seemed very disturbing to me. They were creatures totally different to anything known or imaginable on earth. They were several miles long—and they were alive.

Deep inside me, I knew they were cherubs. Four cherubs were around the throne of God. I wondered if there were other cherubs and where they would be. I remembered that Satan is considered a fallen cherub[23] and that God had placed cherubim to guard the entrance to the Garden of Eden.

"After he drove the man out, he placed on the east side of the Garden of Eden cherubim and a flaming sword flashing back and forth to guard the way to the tree of life" (Genesis 3:24).

I knew that the time had not yet come for me to take a closer look at these creatures.

The shell of the throne room, the shining vault, caught my interest, and I looked at it more closely. I was surprised to find that it

---

23 Ezekiel 28:14

consisted of living beings, of angels. These angels looked like the image I had in my mind of classical angel images. They were shining brightly. The golden light emanated from their whole bodies. They were arranged at completely equal distances from one another, forming the entire outer shell of the sphere out of millions and millions of living beings.

The shell reminded me of a structure made up of individual hexagons. However, the angels were arranged without any separating grid or anything constructed. They floated in space, next to each other. I saw that they were touching at the corners of the imaginary hexagons and were arrayed perfectly side by side. Since I had the impression that they were not much bigger than me, there must have been billions of these beings forming the gigantic surface of the shell.

"Then I looked and heard the voice of many angels, numbering thousands upon thousands, and ten thousand times ten thousand. They encircled the throne and the living creatures and the elders" (Revelation 5:11).

"Spread out above the heads of the living creatures was what looked like an expanse, sparkling like ice, and awesome" (Ezekiel 1:22).

"I saw the Lord sitting on his throne with all the host of heaven standing round him on his right and on his left" (see 1 Kings 22:19).

CHAPTER 45

At the Outer Shell

Two days later, the picture of the shining angels that were forming the outer shell became more specific. With Jesus as my companion, I was able to approach the shell very closely and saw that all the angels remained completely fixed in their positions. We were directly in front of one of the angels, so close that I was able to talk to him. This particular angel was wearing a shining robe, had wings and a human face; he reminded me of the commonly known representations of angels, just that the wings were completely different. They did not look at all like bird wings, as far as their bodily structure was concerned. Instead, they seemed to be made of light. The angel had a very majestic appearance and radiated a great calmness that words cannot really describe.

Jesus encouraged me to ask the angel about his name, and he readily told me what it was. It was too long for me to retain. I asked him for the meaning of the name, and it was something like, "One who will look upon the glory of the Lord forever and will praise Him for all eternity." He told me that every angel in this shell had a similar name.

"For I tell you that their angels in heaven always see the face of my Father in heaven" (see Matthew 18:10).

I noticed once again the geometrical position of this angel and of all the ones around him. He was positioned inside an imaginary, regular hexagon. The angel was about 10 feet tall. The imaginary hexagon had a height of 13 feet. The angel had six wings made of a light-like substance. The wings didn't move, even when he was talking to me. They came out from his back. Two of them were bent around his head and covered it, crossing one another. Since the wings were made of something like a transparent surface of light, they were see-through. Both wings pointed with their tips exactly to the two upper corners of the hexagon. Two of the other wings pointed, like outstretched arms, to the middle corners of the hexagon, and the remaining two wings bent from behind around the lower body, covering it also, crossing one another, and reached towards the two lower corners of the hexagon. The surrounding angels were standing in the same position inside the imaginary honeycomb grid, so that each wingtip of an angel was touching the wingtip of another angel. Each angel was surrounded by six others.

The whole picture was totally perfect and peaceful. The angels glowed with a gentle golden shimmer. They radiated, so that even the empty space between them was filled with light. I was not able to see through these gaps or distinguish what was lying behind them.

I asked him if he always maintained this position, and he answered that he would fill this space for all eternity. It was what he had been created for, and everything he desired was to be here, in the presence of the glory of God, as a precious and irreplaceable building stone of the heavenly throne room. I was amazed. This angel will be in this position for all eternity, and it provides him total satisfaction. It is the purpose and meaning of his existence.

> **In the year that King Uzziah died, I saw the Lord seated on a throne, high and exalted, and the train of his robe filled the temple. Above him were seraphs, each with six wings: With two wings they covered their faces, with two they covered their feet, and with two they were flying. And they were calling to one another:**
>
> **"Holy, holy, holy is the Lord Almighty; the whole earth is full of his glory" (Isaiah 6:1-3).**

CHAPTER 46

Above the Throne

During the early morning hours of a prayer night, while we were worshipping quietly, I became aware that I was once again inside the heavenly throne room. I moved closer to the throne and soon came to be on the top edge of one of the outer discs, just above the round backrest.

In the middle part of the circular surface was the gigantic opening from the center which flowed the living stream. The diameter of the stream was much smaller than the diameter of the opening. I went to the rim and noticed that it was not simply an enormous hole, but rather a crater-like opening that steadily became narrower below. The opening was so large that on earth one would have hardly been able to see the other side. Similar to an antique amphitheater, steps were leading downwards. They were completely regular and formed a big, perfect ring inside the huge circle.

All the steps were made of the same blunt material as the throne, and I bent down to take a closer look at them. To my surprise I noticed that the throne was in fact made of nothing else than solid gold. This material that seemed so blunt to my eyes was pure gold! In the midst of the glory of the throne room it seemed dull and blunt, compared to the heavenly reality. I was so surprised that I called out audibly, "Wow, this is made of gold!" Deep inside of me, I was aware that this gold represented the righteous deeds of the saints. That is the praise upon which the Lord is enthroned.

"Yet you are holy, enthroned on the praises of Israel" (Psalm 22:3, ESV).

I moved down towards the area where the living stream was flowing out, and I floated downwards over the numerous steps. Below, I found a large, perfectly round opening, out of which the glowing stream was literally gushing with great force and speed. It was very impressive and inspiring to look at.

"Like a pent-up flood that the breath of the Lord drives along" (see Isaiah 59:19).

Jesus said that I should not put my hand into the stream, because otherwise I would be instantly carried away with it. This made me think of the Scripture verse:

"Because those who are led by the Spirit of God are sons of God" (Romans 8:14).

Surrounding the area at the center of the big circle—evoking rather a gigantic waterfall than a source, even though it was streaming upward, not downward, from my perspective—there was, on the lowest step, something like an ornamental, glass-like parapet, which looked nearly like a handrail.

From below, from the bottom of the funnel, I looked up. It was a strange picture. The steps reminded me of an amphitheater and seemed much steeper from this perspective than from above. I was able to clearly see the whole of the round rim of the huge opening. To my surprise, I did not see the glowing angels of the expanse behind it, but a starry night sky, like something you would see on earth on a clear night. I found this very confusing.

Looking up from the lowest step, I noticed a small detail on the level of where the stream of the Holy Spirit came out. Four small canals, like pipes, were going through the golden base of the throne in all four "cardinal directions," leading from the center to the outer side of the base. The diameter of each was small, I guess about one yard at the most. I did not see anything flowing through them. These four pipes formed two perpendicular axes. Suddenly, I found myself high above the throne and was able to see that these axes were pointing directly to the four cherub-beings.

These cherubs caught my interest, but I knew that the time had still not come for me to take a closer look at them. However, I became aware of something concerning their nature. The cherubs are the powers of the created universe, the controlling powers of creation. They represent the divine world order. A cherub is a universal power. Satan also had been a cherub once. In his rebellion against God, he seeks to establish his own universal world order.

In a flash, I was once again inside the "crater" with Jesus standing at my side. We were moving upward and ended up standing on the edge of the opening. I saw hundreds of trees growing in regular intervals all around the opening. They were all different, and each one was planted in a huge container or tub. These tubs were all different as well and harmonized in a fitting way with the trees they contained. In the space I could see, they seemed like fruit trees, at the most about 30 feet high. However, as said before, human measures seem to be inadequate in this heavenly context.

The image faded slowly, and I heard a person in the meeting I was participating in read a passage from the Bible out loud. It was a passage from the book of Ezekiel and talked about the cherubs and the stream flowing out from the throne of God.

"You who sit enthroned between the cherubim, shine forth" (see Psalm 80:1).

CHAPTER 47

Beside the Golden Stream

During a long prayer walk, I found myself inside the heavenly throne room. Jesus was there, right next to me. As He had already done many times, He asked me if I was ready to see something new. I answered, "Yes!" and He led me to the other side of the throne.

We were approaching the living stream in the center area between the throne and the outer shell. It was gushing at great speed right next to us. The river had a dynamic and power that was fascinating, downright shattering. There is nothing on earth that could compare with it. It really was mighty, full of supernatural, unearthly might. We were able to look deep into the golden-transparent substance, which looked like moving flames of fire mixed with crystal-like, golden resin.

Jesus told me that I could now touch the stream. With the palm of my hand, I very carefully and slowly touched the quickly flowing substance. I didn't put my hand straight into it, but let it glide alongside my hand. When I looked at my hand the moment after, it was glistening and golden. The stream had left some of its gold on my hand. Later, I discovered a Bible passage which touched me in a particular way. Zechariah describes the heavenly throne room with the stream of the Spirit flowing in two directions, in an unusual vision.

"So he said to me ... 'Not by might nor by power, but by my Spirit,' says the Lord Almighty.... Again I asked him, What are these two olive branches beside the two gold pipes that pour out golden oil?" (see Zechariah 4:6-12)

The next day, the picture was revealed further. I was once again in the heavenly throne room. The stream of the Holy Spirit flowed in two directions from the throne of God, through the golden, sphere-shaped room, and disappeared on each side through the openings at the zenith of the vault. I gave some thought to the way the heavenly river was flowing, which did not fit how I had imagined it before, and then I realized I was beginning to understand something.

"Then the angel showed me the river of the water of life, as clear as crystal, flowing from the throne of God and of the Lamb" (Revelation 22:1).

I had already wondered where this river was flowing. Now I understood that this river of blessings, flowing in two directions, was something which was coming out of both arms and hands of the body of Jesus. The body of Jesus—the born-again people, the church—is us. Jesus told us that out of our bodies would flow streams of living water. Through the laying on of hands and blessing, these streams of God are flowing like liquid gold from heaven out of our innermost being, through our body and our hands.

"Whoever believes in me, as the Scripture has said, streams of living water will flow from within him. By this he meant the Spirit" (see John 7:38-39).

The river of the Holy Spirit wants to flow out of our innermost being. God wants to sit on the throne of the inner man, in each of His children, and wants to establish the kingdom of God in them. The inner man of each born-again Christian is, in a certain sense, the throne room of God.

"Don't you know that you yourselves are God's temple and that God's Spirit lives in you?" (1 Corinthians 3:16).

The Spirit of God dwells completely in a person who has been born again. Therefore, we also have all the knowledge, all the power, all the joy, and all the love of God. At the same time, He also dwells in millions of other children, flows out of the heavenly throne, burns in the seven torches, and has eyes that range throughout the earth.[24] He is not limited by the boundaries of our human understanding. He is God.

The question is whether we allow Him to really sit on the throne of our lives, and whether we agree that He can work through us. The question is how much liberty and room we will give Him, so that He can flow out of us towards a dying world.

Then I saw myself close to this golden, gushing stream again. I knew that if I were to put my hand into it, it would carry me beyond the expanse of the throne room at a great speed, toward something completely unknown. But I also knew that the moment had come for me to be carried away by the stream of God. So, I courageously stretched my hand into the stream and was carried away instantly at great speed. I did not see anything and did not notice at which moment I was going through the golden shell of the throne room. After a while I noticed that I was in a large earthly room with oriental flair. I then witnessed in complete detail the raising of a wealthy person from the dead in a North African country. I did not know whether this was happening at the time I saw it, or whether it was a vision of something that was to happen in the future.

"You give them drink from your river of delights. For with you is the fountain of life; in your light we see light" (see Psalm 36:8-9).

"The wind blows wherever it pleases. You hear its sound, but you cannot tell where it comes from or where it is going. So it is with everyone born of the Spirit" (John 3:8).

---

24 2 Chronicles 16:9

CHAPTER 48

A Torch of Fire

During a gentle and calm prayer night, the fourth chapter of the book of Revelation was read out.

> **"After this I looked, and behold, a door standing open in heaven!... and behold, a throne stood in heaven, with one seated on the throne.... Around the throne were twenty-four thrones, and seated on the thrones were twenty-four elders, clothed in white garments, with golden crowns on their heads. From the throne came flashes of lightning, and rumblings and peals of thunder, and before the throne were burning seven torches of fire, which are the seven spirits of God, and before the throne there was as it were a sea of glass, like crystal. And around the throne, on each side of the throne, are four living creatures, full of eyes in front and behind" (see Revelation 4:1-6, ESV).**

Once again, I found myself inside the throne room, diagonally above the throne, close to the golden shell. From my viewpoint, the stream of the Spirit flowed upward and downward from the throne. Suddenly, my position changed. I turned 90 degrees to one side, and the whole picture turned at the same time. I was now directly in front of the throne that rose vertically before me, and the river of the Holy Spirit flowed toward the right and the left. I was positioned in front of the middle "disc" of the throne, which rose before me, and whose curves disappeared toward the back on top and at the bottom.[25]

25 I would like to mention that regarding everything I experienced in this unearthly, unnatural, sphere-shaped

Directly in front of me, just before the throne itself, there was a torch burning brightly, floating in space. I knew that its name was "wisdom." In the middle, it had something like a pipe clamp made of gold, which to my surprise was bejeweled, like an earthly crown. White fire blazed out from it in both directions. It was nearly like a symbolic miniature of the throne. I knew that all around the throne were seven of those torches. I was not sure of its size in relation to the other elements. Compared to the mightily rising throne, it seemed relatively small to me, which surprised me also. But then I understood once again certain things.

"Then I saw a Lamb, looking as if it had been slain, standing in the center of the throne, encircled by the four living creatures and the elders. He had seven horns and seven eyes, which are the seven spirits of God sent out into all the earth" (Revelation 5:6).

The book of Revelation describes the Lamb of God. It has seven eyes, representing the seven Spirits of God. Since the torches also represent the seven Spirits of God, there must be a deeper connection between the eyes of the divine Lamb and the torches of fire around the throne of God.

"And his eyes were like blazing fire" (see Revelation 1:13-14).

Spiritual vision and spiritual discernment are like spiritual fire, like brightly shining light. Jesus said that the eyes are the lamps of the body.

"The eye is the lamp of the body. If your eyes are good, your whole body will be full of light" (Matthew 6:22).

---

room, any attempt at spatial orientation seems completely inadequate. I was moving around the throne room like an astronaut floating in space, without any awareness of up and down, right and left, front and back. If I use these terms, they refer simply to my momentary perspective.

I understood that this had a deeper meaning than I had grasped up until now. I noted for myself, *Holy Spirit = Fire = Light = Eyes = Knowledge.*

Only when the Holy Spirit opens the eyes of our heart and gives us enlightened eyes of the heart[26] can we gain access to understanding divine circumstances. As followers of Jesus, we should keep the fire of the Spirit burning[27], and live and move on in spiritual knowledge.

Then, Jesus started talking to me. He said that it is important and significant to understand that spiritual fire is the same as spiritual eyes and spiritual vision. This was the foundation for the things He wanted to show me next. He said that the seven spirits of God mentioned in Isaiah designated seven ways of the Holy Spirit operating, but there is in reality only one Spirit. This was more significant than a human being could comprehend.

"The Spirit of the Lord will rest on him—the Spirit of wisdom and of understanding, the Spirit of counsel and of power, the Spirit of knowledge and of the fear of the Lord" (Isaiah 11:2).

The Holy Spirit can dwell simultaneously in millions of believers and still be one Spirit. He has the same unlimited power and effect in each person. While the Holy Spirit is burning as seven torches near the throne, at the same time He is the stream flowing out of the throne of God. This spiritual truth is completely beyond anything that could be described by a human picture. The Holy Spirit is God. And God transcends all understanding.

---

26 Ephesians 1:18
27 Romans 12:11

CHAPTER 49

Worship Before the Throne

During a morning worship time, I found myself once again unexpectedly inside the throne room. I recognized that I was next to the golden shell. The room was huge, but I could clearly and distinctly see every detail. I perceived the shell, the massive throne in the center, the armies of people and angels, and the stream of God. I moved over to one of the twenty-four white thrones which surrounded the golden throne in equal intervals. Jesus was next to me.

First, I stayed at the base of the small throne, and then I moved slowly toward the top. In this way I reached the person sitting on this throne. I knew inside that it was Stephen. He said that he wanted to show me how to worship the Lord. Straight away, I found myself in a similar position to his and had my face turned toward the throne rising massively in front of us and filling nearly all our field of vision. The centerpiece of the throne stood vertically directly in front of us.

Parallel to both directions in which the stream flowed out, I lifted my arms to both sides of the throne, toward the Father and toward the Son, Jesus Christ, and let the Holy Spirit flow out of my mouth through worship. That is the heart of worship: the Father and the Son receive the worship which the Holy Spirit causes to flow through us, the children of God. Then, the picture became blurred and blended into a time of worship.

In the following weeks, during worship times, I saw the gigantic golden throne rising in the same way in front of me. When I looked to the right or to the left, I could see the bright river of the Holy Spirit flowing in the distance, and even further behind, the golden shell.

Often, I stretched out my arms in both directions of the river and worshiped God. But I still was not able to see the one sitting on the throne.

During such a time of worship I came closer to the golden throne, so close that I was able to touch it. I reverently remained there for some time, and then I turned so that I came to stand with my back to the throne, looking toward the vast room. There were the delicate and filigree-looking armies of humans and angels, the thrones of the ancient ones, and the four cherubs. Everything was clothed in warm golden light. I found it fascinating how everything was floating freely in space while, at the same time, maintaining a fixed, perfect position.

Sometime later, I became aware what a privilege it was to be granted to see the glory of this overwhelming room, which is so unexpectedly different and beyond human imagination. Still, I was conscious that all this was only a picture suited for me personally, so that I could, in some way, grasp and comprehend it with my limited understanding. What I saw was just one of the facets of a complexity and dimension beyond anything a human being could understand. It only was a tiny piece of the glory, one single angle, a tiny spark of what God has prepared for us.

The throne room of God is not a room one could ever comprehend with earthly intelligence. It is divine, eternal, sublime, and completely transcends our understanding. God revealed these things to me in a certain way, and I can relate and describe them at least partly with my words. Nevertheless, these words only scratch the surface of the true spiritual reality; they are nothing more than patchwork.

"For we know in part and we prophesy in part, but when perfection comes, the imperfect disappears" (1 Corinthians 13:9-10).

CHAPTER 50

The Eye of the Cherub

I woke up during the night and found myself in the heavenly throne room, far up above the throne. I could see everything clearly and noticed the trees which were standing on the backrest of the throne, like a green string of pearls in perfect order. Even though they were relatively big, they were planted in buckets which were at least as tall as man and, to my surprise, apparently filled with ordinary earth. The buckets themselves were all different, but all made of gold.

Jesus, who was standing at my side, asked me if I would like to look at the cherubs. I answered "Yes," and straight away I found myself in front of one of these totally unearthly creatures.

This being was of an overwhelming size and reminded me of a huge, horizontal pipe. I had the impression that this being was several miles long, with a diameter of several hundred yards, perhaps even up to one mile. I felt as if I was standing on a small hill directly in front of the very large entrance to an immense cave. It was very strange, disconcerting, and could not be compared with anything on earth.

"O Lord Almighty, God of Israel, enthroned between the cherubim" (see Isaiah 37:16).

After some time, I noticed a sound. It was a sustained, deep sound, without any vibrations or modifications. It belonged to this creature. I could look right inside this strange body. The term "pipe-like" did not fit, because the being was not open at both ends, but the back end was somehow closed. Inside, it was like a cave and became steadily narrower until it was nothing more than a point. I thought about this center point and realized that an imagined axis reached from this point to the cherub on the other side of the throne, passing right through the middle of the throne. The four cherubs were carrying two imagined axes that crossed right in the center of the throne, in the Holy of Holies, at the mercy seat of God.

"The cherubim spread their wings over the place of the ark and overshadowed the ark and its carrying poles" (1 Kings 8:7).

I asked Jesus if I could go into the opening before me, so to speak right into the being itself. Jesus answered that it was possible, but that it would be terrifying for me, because in doing so, I would enter a place of total revelation about myself.

So, I moved around the unearthly creature instead and looked at it from the outside. It was totally covered with a bizarre, shiny skin, which was blunt at the same time. To take a closer look at its consistency, I moved to the edge and inspected this unusual surface. The blunt skin appeared rather dark in the golden light of the throne room.

I knew from the Bible that the book of Revelation describes the cherubim as covered over and over with eyes. I could not see anything of the sort. The surface was completely even outside as well as inside the "cave."

"In the center, around the throne, were four living creatures, and they were covered with eyes, in front and behind" (see Revelation 4:6).

Suddenly, I understood this surface was "eye"! The skin of the being consisted of "eye." Earthly beings are limited to their actual eyes serving as sensory and perceptual organs, but the whole surface of the creature functioned this way. Everything on the outside of this being was one single, eye-like, sensory organ. What I also understood immediately was that it was not just an eye in the sense of having earthly visual abilities, but it was a spiritual eye capable of a much wider range of discernment.

"Each of the four living creatures had six wings and was covered with eyes all around, even under his wings. Day and night they never stop saying: Holy, holy, holy is the Lord God Almighty, who was, and is, and is to come" (Revelation 4:8).

I understood what the description in Revelation tried to convey. The whole surface of this living creature, all around and internally, outside and inside, consisted entirely of "eye."

I pondered what the eye on the inside of the creature could actually see. It looks at the eye on the other side of itself; it is constantly contemplating itself. To enter there and to be looked at constantly with total spiritual discernment must indeed be terrifying. If the sustained gaze of another person can already be destabilizing and disconcerting for us, how much more the gaze of this spiritual being!

After a while, I noticed that this being did not seem to have wings or anything of the kind. Straight after this, I found myself high above the throne, very close to the outer golden shell.

For the first time since I was granted these visits to the throne room, I was able to discern a few bright surfaces which had been very difficult to distinguish due to the abundance of golden light. They looked like totally even surfaces, like layers of light. They extended on the level of the throne, between the cherubim. The edges of these triangular surfaces of light were curved and pointed at the ends. Two of those surfaces went out from each cherub, and I recognized them as being their "wings." They touched the tips of the ones coming from the next cherub. These wings were made of a different substance than the bodies of the cherubs; they were made of light, or something very similar to it. It was possible to move through them without difficulty. The surfaces reminded me somewhat of the light shining through a canopy of green leaves on a summer's day, forming a sort of fan or veil of light.

"He placed the cherubim inside the innermost room of the temple, with their wings spread out. The wing of one cherub touched one wall, while the wing of the other touched the other wall, and their wings touched each other in the middle of the room" (1 Kings 6:27).

These filigree wings seemed strange to me, as it was such a stark contrast to the heavy bodies of the cherubim. I could not make out where exactly the wings were coming out of the bodies of the cherubim. In any case, they were nothing like the classical images of angels' wings with which we are familiar.

Each one of the living creatures had two wings reaching out horizontally, on the same level as the throne. Then, I saw that each cherub had two more wings reaching out vertically. They were made exactly the same way, but were much bigger, reaching up to the river of the Spirit.

Then I turned my attention to the front openings of the beings, which were facing the throne. Out of these round openings also, there were wings of light coming out toward the top and the bottom. However, they were not flat, but had a curved, spherical surface, a bit like the outside of a funnel. They reminded me of the terms "shade" and "shield," both found in the Bible and designating spiritual protection. From each cherub, there were two of those wings of light, pointing toward the top and bottom of the throne. At the meeting point of these shields, they formed a neat, regular edge. These eight light structures formed a sphere-shaped covering all around the throne.

In my mind I heard it said that the cherubim were protecting and shielding. They protect the throne of God and, in a certain sense, uphold it. It made me think of the old German hymn "Jesus Christus herrscht als König" ("Jesus Christ Reigns as King")[28] where it says:

28 Words: Philipp Friedrich Hiller, 1757; music: Johan Löhner, 1691 – English translation by the translator of this book.

Principalities and powers
Forces that keep watch over the throne
Give Him all the glory
All dominions there in heaven,
And here in our earthly turmoil,
Are prepared to serve Him.

God is the Lord, the Lord is One
And no one is like Him
Only the Son is His equal,
Whose seat cannot be overthrown
Whose life cannot be put out
Whose reign is an eternal reign.

Equal in power and equal in honor
He sits beneath gentle choirs
Above all the cherubim
To the ends of this world and of the heavens
He has everything in His hands,
For the Father gave it to Him.

Cherubim are beings that shield the throne of God, the central place of the presence of the Lord; they "keep watch over the throne" and block the access to the presence of God.

I then pondered the nature of those beings and found myself immediately in front of the cherub. I knew that it was the one who is compared to an ox, or calf, in the book of Revelation. How this comparison to an earthly animal came about was beyond my comprehension. I saw neither head, nor face, nor anything that looked in the slightest like an ox, or anything resembling an animal at all.

"The first living creature was like a lion, the second was like an ox, the third had a face like a man, the fourth was like a flying eagle" (Revelation 4:7).

Two days later, I was standing once again in a vision before this cherub. I looked into the huge, tunnel-like opening and heard the deep sound. I addressed the being and asked, "Why are you described as an ox in Revelation?" The answer of the creature came directly to my mind and pointed me to Him who really matters: "Do not ask me; ask Jesus. I am only a cherub, but He is God, worthy of praise in all eternity!"

CHAPTER 51

The Cherubim

Once again, I found myself high up in the heavenly throne room. Jesus was close by my side. He pointed out to me that the room was much, much larger than I remembered it to be. It was huge. I recognized inwardly that the middle "disc" of the throne alone must have measured several miles in height.

I looked around for a while at things that I had seen before, mainly the four cherubim, the armies of men, and the shell made of myriads of angels, forming what seemed like one solid gold surface. I could not see the wings of the cherubim, or at least I did not detect them.

Far below us was the cherub that the Bible described as an ox, a young bull. Jesus asked me if I wanted Him to explain this to me, and I immediately said yes. At once I was directly before the heavenly creature, which to me still looked more like an object than a living being. I contemplated the surface made of this shimmering, iridescent eye-surface and found myself standing right in front of the opening of the being, rising for several miles before me. That was my impression. This was very strange and weird, although not frightening. This creature was simply different—and I knew that it was exceedingly powerful.

I understood inwardly that the ox was an animal for sacrifice, and therefore clean, which interestingly enough is not the case of the eagle and the lion, to which two of the other cherubim are likened.

An ox is strong and normally not aggressive, but good-natured and peaceful. When he fights, however, he is boiling, quick-tempered, fierce, impetuous, and will break through or run down everything that gets in his way. He will crush his adversaries and his aggressors, knocking them over and trampling them down. When he fights, he breaks through with mighty, instinctive force, without thinking, without ruse. In many pagan religions, oxen or bulls were worshipped and venerated because they represent in their nature the real, existing power of a cherub. Of course, a cherub is not an ox, but a universal, spiritual force, one of the controlling powers of creation, representing the divine world order. But the principle of this being is, for human, earthly comprehension, best represented through the image of the ox or a bull.

Nevertheless, I was surprised that the Bible compares these mighty creatures to normal earthly animals. But then I recognized that this comparison can be likened to the fact that a human being is sometimes compared to an ape. To do this is in a certain limited way, correct and coherent, since there is no better earthly comparison; even though we know that it is not correct. A human is incomparably more than an ape, but at the same time, the ape is the animal that is the most like a human. It works in a similar way with the cherubim and the animals to which they are compared. These animals illustrate a small portion of their nature.

Another of the cherubim is described as a flying eagle—not resting or sitting. An eagle soars above all else. In a certain sense, he has no enemies and descends now and then from far up high to grab his prey. The lion, however, instills fear simply by his presence. He is conscious of his power and position and expresses it by his roar. He rips and tears his opponents to pieces. The man, to which the last cherub is likened, has comparably little strength of his own. But through the position and authority given to him by God, he is far more powerful than any animal could ever be. And so it is with the cherub. I realized that the one who is symbolized by a man is the mightiest of the four, followed by the lion, the eagle and, in the last position, the ox.

While I was still pondering all this, a voice told me to look.

So, I looked into the cave-like depth of the cherub. Suddenly, I noticed that the being was full of light, right until the very depth of it, and that there were no shadows cast anywhere. In the same second, I realized also that there were no cast shadows in the entire throne room. Absolutely everything was bathing in soft, golden light. The only thing glowing intensely from the inside was the river of the Spirit flowing through the throne room.

I looked back at the cherub and was horrified, because suddenly, from deep inside, growing bigger by the second, a mighty, incredibly huge wild bull was storming head down towards me. He was clearly visible, clear-cut, but was not made of the same material as the other things I had seen in this throne room so far. He seemed to consist of light. This mighty bull disappeared in the tube, just seconds before he would have reached me.

Now, I was completely confused.

CHAPTER 52

A Man from the Host

After a long period of time, I found myself again in the heavenly throne room. I saw the mighty, golden expanse dressing itself high above me like a gigantic dome. I realized that I was standing right next to a person, a man standing in the rear left corner of one of the "hosts" that were visible everywhere inside the heavenly throne room.

I looked above me and saw other similar networks made up of millions of people at a great distance, who were standing and worshipping in the presence of God. Looking below, I saw the same picture. I looked in front, toward the throne, and saw thousands of people standing in rank and file before me. They formed the left outer edge of this host. Everyone was looking toward the throne. I looked to my right and saw the rear edge of this network, again formed out of thousands of people. I knew instinctively that the network was square-shaped, and that the edges therefore consisted of an equal number of people. Since I had the impression that there must be thousands on each edge, I assumed that the entire network was at least 2,000 by 2,000 people, equaling 4 million people. A real host!

I felt that I should talk to the person standing next to me. He wore a long, brightly shining, white robe with a golden belt and a narrow golden band for a crown. It reminded me of the clothes Jesus wore. The person was barefoot and turned towards me. It was evidently a man who had lived in Asia. I talked to him about what he was doing here in the heavenly throne room, and he explained to me that it was an enormous privilege for him to be part of this throne room. I asked him what it meant to him to stand at the corner point, and he replied that the Lord had granted him the grace to be a pillar of the church. This was symbolized by the place he was occupying. But at the same time, he pointed out to me that each person was of infinite importance. For without each single person present, the throne room would not be perfect.

I talked with him about the fact that uncountable people, or living beings, were standing in worship before God—apparently without ever leaving their position—while I knew at the same time that the heavenly Jerusalem was filled with life and activity, and that the beings in the heavenly places were actively doing something, constantly moving around on behalf of God. How did this fit together?

His answer surprised me. He pointed out to me that I was an earthly human being, and that I was at the same time in my own home and here, in this heavenly place. Both positions were totally real. With my spirit, I was moving in the spiritual reality. With my body, I was in the natural world. This, he said, was similar in the heavenly dimension. While he was standing before God in worship for all eternity, without ever feeling the urge or the desire to leave this position, he was at the same time in the heavenly Jerusalem and at many other places in the heavenly dimension, acting on behalf of God's interests. That which seemed to me nearly static in the throne room was only one small viewpoint of the heavenly reality. I was able to be on earth and, at the same time, in heaven and in the same way the heavenly beings could be in different places at the same time in the Spirit. In the Spirit, there are no limitations in space or time. This would be something that was beyond human comprehension. He was forever here and forever at many other different places. God was forever here on His throne and forever omnipresent. Even though I was able to comprehend his answer, it left me with a strange feeling. Once again, something was far beyond my limited, earthly way of seeing things up to now.

Then Jesus, who was standing on the other side of me, put His arm around my shoulder and said:

"Heaven is beyond any human imagination. Any description

of heaven is nothing more than a small fragment and shows a minute detail. Believe Me, heaven is totally different. It is the constant, eternal, everlasting dwelling in the presence of the almighty, all-knowing, unlimited God. You, as a human, have been taken into all that He is and has. The inheritance of the "saints in the kingdom of light" is much, much more than a person could ever imagine. Whoever does not take hold of this inheritance has missed out on life itself. You will be amazed for all eternity about what God has done and prepared for you as a person. God has prepared something truly divine for His children. There will never be a moment of regret, boredom, or doubt. Nobody will ever wish to be elsewhere."

CHAPTER 53

Into the Throne Itself

One morning, I was talking to the Lord about these pictures and visions while lying in my bed. He told me that I could come anytime and continue looking, and that there was nothing that could hinder me from doing so, except myself. I could move freely in the area of the vision. It was entirely up to me how much I would see.

"Set your hearts on things above, where Christ is seated at the right hand of God. Set your minds on things above, not on earthly things" (see Colossians 3:1-2).

Then, I suddenly was once again in the throne room. I felt that Jesus was next to me to guide me. Far below us was the throne. In the same way as I had already perceived it before many times, the surface of the throne seemed to be dull and matte compared to the surroundings bathed in golden shining light.

Unexpectedly, a glimmer of light moved across the throne. It reminded me of the shine of a torch illuminating an object when it is carried passed it, or of the rays of a rising sun caressing something. The throne began to shine, as if it was floodlighted. The beam went slowly across it, and it looked different than before. Now I noticed another object that was beaming, shining, fiery and yet completely in harmony with itself. Then the voice of Jesus resounded, "Take a look at it!"

Straight away, I was in the middle section, on the same level as the torches and the thrones of the ancient ones, very close before the throne. It rose directly in front of me and deep below me, like a wall.

I looked a little bit to the right and to the left and saw the huge curvature, disappearing slowly from my view towards the back.

The throne in front of me was made this time of a shining substance, difficult to describe. It was not like the gold that I had seen up to now. Its appearance reminded me of a calmly burning, static flame, a little like the substance I had seen in the heavenly Jerusalem. It was solid, but not in the way earthly matter is solid. It glowed from the inside out. It was a warm glow, and into my thoughts came the words, "higher than Mount Everest." Then, Jesus invited me, "Go inside!"

I was surprised. This invitation came totally unexpectedly. I stood directly in front of the throne, barely at an arm's length. After a short hesitation, I stretched out my hand and touched it. In doing this, my hand slid into it, as if plunging into thick fog. There was no sensation of resistance. Suddenly, I was moving completely inside this substance; I literally slid through it. This was an experience that is difficult to describe. It was different to that which I had experienced at the pearly gate because I felt very clearly how the substance was also going through me—and at the same time, I was going through it. I was reminded of underwater photos depicting beams of light going through the water.

The golden substance of the throne was in no way changed by the fact that I was moving through it. If it had been fog, it would have moved, but this was not the case here. As soon as I had gone inside, I didn't feel anything except its warm, glowing light. It surrounded and penetrated me; I was completely flooded by it.

I felt without orientation and confused, but Jesus invited me, "Keep going!" I moved forward a little bit several times but paused again and again. Then, the picture faded.

CHAPTER 54

At the Place of Origin

During a day of fasting, I noticed that Jesus was standing right next to me. We were surrounded by complete darkness. I knew that we were inside a closed room. We were not standing on the floor but floating inside this room. Sometimes it is possible to get a feeling for proportions and size, even in dark rooms, but here, it was impossible. I could not tell how big or small the room was.

While we were there, Jesus explained that we were in a room right inside the golden throne. This place was the origin of all things. Since I was cleansed by His blood, the blood of the perfect sacrificial Lamb, I was allowed to approach this room and move around in it.

"In him [Jesus] **and through faith in him we may approach God with freedom and confidence" (Ephesians 3:12).**

I couldn't see anything, but I noticed that a gentle scent and a soft sound filled the room. I did not move or speak, for with my whole being I felt that this room could only be described with one word: holy! The center of the Holy of Holies!

A few days later, I was once again in the dark room in the center of the throne. I held the hand of Jesus, who stood beside me. He told me that I could come here for prayer and intercession, right into the presence of God. In times following this, I often stood in this room during prayer times, with Jesus directly at my side. At one point I realized that the room must be round, just like the golden throne.

Then I remembered the four small tunnels. They went through the entire throne and pointed in direction of the four living creatures. I thought about the two poles of the ark of the covenant, which were passed through rings to carry it. Invisible "poles" that would have been passed through these tunnels would cross right here in this central room. I instinctively knew that the river of the Holy Spirit had its origin right here in this room.

I then pondered the fact that the earthly temple was nothing else than the imperfect image of the heavenly truth. The tabernacle and the temple represent a shadow of the eternal reality.

"For Christ did not enter a man-made sanctuary that was only a copy of the true one; he entered heaven itself, now to appear for us in God's presence" (Hebrews 9:24).

I understood that in the heavenly dimension, there were also outer courts, the outer temple buildings, the inner sanctuary, the golden Holy Place, and finally the inner room inside the mercy seat. The tabernacle built by Moses is based on the model, which God had revealed to him in the heavenly places:

"The Lord said to Moses ... let them make me a sanctuary, that I may dwell in their midst. "Exactly as I show you concerning the pattern of the tabernacle, and of all its furniture, so you shall make it" (Exodus 25:1, 8-9 ESV).

I became aware that the "golden room" represented the Holy of Holies. In the temple, the Holy of Holies had been a room, which was totally covered, "shrouded" in a certain sense, in gold.

"So he overlaid the whole interior with gold.... He also covered the floors of both the inner and outer rooms of the temple with gold" (see 1 Kings 6:22, 30).

Inside this room was the place of the ark itself, the place of the mercy seat, which was watched over and covered by the cherubim. Here was the place where God revealed His deepest, innermost being. Underneath the mercy seat, inside the ark of the covenant, was a small, closed space that was never opened. It was a hidden space beneath the atonement covering. Here, the tablets of the law, Aaron's staff that had budded, and a jar of manna were kept.[29]

"Let us then approach the throne of grace with confidence" (see Hebrews 4:16).

Once, after I had finished preparing a sermon, the Lord spoke again to me about the heavenly throne room and explained some more details. In the center of the earthly sanctuary was the Holy of Holies, a closed-up room with no direct access. It was impossible to enter it or to look into it from the outside. In order to recognize something, one had to be inside the room. If you went out from there, you reached the Holy Place, the temple itself, the different courtyards, then the city of Jerusalem, and finally the entire land of the promise.

I had been allowed to see the throne room, the Holy of Holies, and therefore I was, so to speak, inside this closed-up, golden room. Up to now, I did not know what was beyond the golden shell. If this room was the representation of the Holy of Holies, then it must be surrounded by other different areas of heaven, which would correspond to the Holy Place, the temple, the courtyards, etc.

So I asked, "Is the throne room situated inside the heavenly Jerusalem?"

The answer of Jesus was, "Yes! The throne room of God is the center of the heavenly Jerusalem. Just as the Holy of Holies was the center of the camp of the Israelites in the desert, and later of the earthly Jerusalem."

29 Hebrews 9:4

He told me that I had entered this room because I eagerly desired to see the glory of God, to stand before His throne, and to come into His immediate presence. All the children of God had free access to it. Through the saving blood of Jesus, each of us can have unhindered, immediate access to God, even to the Holy of Holies, but most Christians don't reach out for it and will therefore not enter into it. Many will come, but they will stop in one of the outer courts without going any further.

I looked down on me and noticed that I was clothed in a linen robe and that I was barefoot.

A few days later, the Lord revealed to me that the picture of the temple, as it is described in the Bible, is not just a representation of the heavenly reality, but also a representation of the nature of a born-again person. We are called the temple of the Holy Spirit. The composition and the structure of the temple are therefore also a picture of us as God's children:

"But he who unites himself with the Lord is one with him in spirit.... Do you not know that your body is a temple of the Holy Spirit, who is in you, whom you have received from God? You are not your own" (1 Corinthians 6:17, 19).

The actual temple building is a representation of our body. It is visible to everyone; it is our exterior being. The area in front of the temple, into which people can look if the doors are open, is the Holy Place. It represents our soul, which is our mind, our will, and our emotions. Deeper still inside is our spirit. It is represented by the Holy of Holies. Hidden in it, deep down inside for no one to see or to reach, is the place of the ark of the covenant, where He lives in us, the place of His throne and of His glory. It is the place where the Holy Spirit has taken up His dwelling in our spirit, where He is present in our lives.

"Jesus replied, If anyone loves me, he will obey my teaching. My Father will love him, and we will come to him and make our home with him" (John 14:23).

All this is surrounded by different outer courts, representing different levels of relationships with other people, depending on how superficial or intimate they are.

CHAPTER 55

In the Center of the Holy of Holies

Rather suddenly and unexpectedly, I found myself standing directly at arm's length in front of the huge throne in the center of the heavenly throne room. My gaze wandered, and I saw far below me the bright, glowing stream of the Spirit. When I looked up, I saw the same picture. Like an axe, the river was cutting through the entire inner space. It was a picture of perfect peace and calm, nearly static. I had this very strong impression: Here is eternity!

I knew that I was supposed to go inside the throne again. So, I moved forward and reached the inside of the throne. The substance reminded me once again of extremely thick fog, but with a clear and sharp shape that seemed "solid." On one hand, the throne had a solid surface which could be touched and felt, and if something would have been put upon or leaned against it, it would have stayed there. On the other hand, I was able to move right through it.

This time, I was surrounded by darkness straight away, but it felt very comfortable. A soft noise filled the whole object. I moved on, and after a long while I felt as if I was soon going to reach the center, the inner center of the Holy of Holies. Very moved, I realized that I was right in the center of the heavenly Holy of Holies, directly before the place of the eternal sacrifice, the eternal atonement. Jesus invited me to seek Him again and again at this place, and to meet Him here. **"Moses approached the thick darkness where God was" (see Exodus 20:21).**

The next day, I saw the same picture and the same starting point. I moved forward and was immediately surrounded by this substance and by warm darkness. While I was still inside this foggy substance, I took Jesus, who was next to me, by the hand. He said, "I am right here with you!" Hand in hand, we entered the innermost room.

I noticed that the entire throne was filled with subtle, scarcely perceptible music, a melody, gentle and soft. After a time, we moved on until we reached the middle of the room. Even though I could not see anything, I had an idea of the proportions of the room. I knew that the room was sphere-shaped. In its geometrical center was an object made of a cool, unidentifiable material. It was smooth, as if it had been polished, and had sharp, distinct edges. The make-up of this room recalled very much the throne room itself, which was also sphere-shaped, with an object—the throne, shaped in a similar way—in the center.

Jesus told me that only a few people would come to the throne of mercy in this way. Angels would not dare to come, even though there were angels also all around this central room. However, they were not looking at it, but were covering their faces.

CHAPTER 56

A Place Where Only A Few Will Come

One night I woke up and heard Jesus asking me if I wanted to see something. I was once again inside the heavenly throne room, very high up, not far from the point where the river of the Spirit flowed out of the room through the shell. Directly below and far away was the throne. I was able to oversee the whole structure of the entire room from my position. All around the mighty throne were the twenty-four smaller thrones, hardly visible from my position. The hosts of men and angels were everywhere, like light webs, positioned in space all around the throne. I saw the wings of light of the cherubim, evenly dividing the room like surfaces of light. Once again, I noticed the gentle, constant sound which filled the whole room.

Then, I noticed that the cherubim were positioned around the throne according to the four cardinal directions. Why do we divide the space around us in four directions? Why not in five or six or eight? Why north, east, south, and west? In the same way, a circle is divided in four right angles of 90 degrees. Also, on the face of a clock, the figures 3, 6, 9, and 12 are often highlighted. They also divide the circle into four parts. This earthly way of dividing this space is a picture of the fact that there are four powers in heaven, four principles, which indicate these directions. It also reminded me of the fact that the Bible speaks several times of four winds.

"And the angel answered and said to me, 'These are going out to the four winds of heaven, after presenting themselves before the Lord of all the earth'" (Zechariah 6:5 ESV).

After some time, I realized that I was once again inside the darkness of the central room of the throne. I felt this time was different from the other times I had been allowed to enter this awe-inspiring room. Indeed, this time I did not only perceive darkness, but after a while I saw kindling flames, like lightning, flickering all around the altar-like object in the middle of the room. They were not like flames of a fire, and did not look like ember either, but rather like electricity, like sparks, like flashes. The entire atmosphere inside the room was charged, as if it was crackling.

"Then God's temple in heaven was opened, and within his temple was seen the ark of his covenant. And there came flashes of lightning, rumblings, peals of thunder, an earthquake and a great hailstorm" (Revelation 11:19).

Shortly after this, during a prayer time, I was seized by the glory and greatness of God when I heard Jesus inviting me, "Come, I will show you something. Look!"

It was dark. My first impression was that there was something like separate fiery coals lying around. They were sphere-shaped heaps, like balls of red-hot lava. Then I noticed flashes darting back and forth between the fiery objects. Quite a number of these red-hot, flaming objects were spread out over a surface, the size of which I could not make out. Between them, a light was moving quickly back and forth. It reminded me a bit of the light spot of a pointer used for presentations.

"He made darkness around him his canopy, thick clouds, a gathering of water. Out of the brightness before him coals of fire flamed forth" (2 Samuel 22:12-13 ESV).

I knew that the Bible talks of fiery stones and of light moving back and forth. So, I asked Jesus what this was. He explained that He had come to this place after His ascension to send out the Holy Spirit. Here was the wellspring of the river of the Spirit. Here the Spirit of God was brooding, and from here it went out.

Then He told me again that this was a place where only few people would come. This was a holy place, a place where human proportions were not applicable.

"The appearance of the living creatures was like burning coals of fire or like torches. Fire moved back and forth among the creatures; it was bright, and lightning flashed out of it" (Ezekiel 1:13).

CHAPTER 57

The Center of the Heavenly Jerusalem

During a prayer time, Jesus asked me to look at the heavenly Jerusalem.

Shortly afterwards, I was looking at the structure from a great distance. On the inside, I could once again see something like a central cube with edges of light, golden and glowing, penetrated and flooded by many other radiating plains, solids, and three-dimensional vaulted surfaces. The whole thing was incredibly complex, intertwined, and hardly describable. The differently shaped objects were flowing into each other and were forming a whole entity in a way I cannot put into words. They were not solid objects, but rather glowing, bright objects of light. I also saw sphere-shaped "light bubbles," which were encompassing the whole figure like a shroud.

I already knew that this perfection could not be grasped with my human mind, limited by space and time. This was the heavenly bride! What a bewildering thought.

Just a moment later, I was unexpectedly inside the heavenly throne room. I saw the throne, the river of the Holy Spirit, and the golden, sphere-shaped shell. Then something happened that I was not prepared for. I suddenly found myself outside the throne room, and for the first time I saw it from the outside, like a golden, glowing sphere. Then I saw how the complex structure of the heavenly Jerusalem and the sphere of the heavenly throne room moved and melted into each other. The pictures of the throne room and the heavenly Zion, which I was already familiar with, became one. It was like objects of light merging together, like a cross fade. Both appearances merged, flowed into each other, connected, and united with one another.

I was completely stunned. Both visions, which had been so different from one another, were suddenly penetrating each other and formed a new entity. In the middle of it all, I saw the throne of God and knew that it was the center of the heavenly Jerusalem.

The unexpected and strange picture impacted me deeply. God had revealed two different heavenly spheres, and now He showed me how the two were related to each other.

"I will make a covenant of peace with them; it will be an everlasting covenant.... and I will put my sanctuary among them forever. My dwelling place will be with them ... when my sanctuary is among them forever" (see Ezekiel 37:26-28).

CHAPTER 58

The River in the City

It was night when I suddenly felt that Jesus was at my side and took me by the hand. For one or two seconds, I had the impression we were flying, then we stood on a very high tower. This tower was lean and spread out sphere-like at the top, like the bud of a flower on top of a stalk or a stem. The tower was entirely made of gold, and I realized that it was situated at the edge of the huge building site inside the heavenly Zion. It was something like an observation platform, and below us spread the construction site of the heavenly Jerusalem, as far as the eye could reach.

It was a construction site made of light, of gold, of glowing—with this indescribable, complex, building-like structure. When we think of a city, we think of it as spreading in a two-dimensional way, in breadth and length. But in this case, it rather evoked an inconceivably huge three-dimensional building; a building with lakes, parks, alleys, streets, dwellings, and much more in it. All this was inconceivably complex and woven into each other in a multi-dimensional way.

Inside of me, I knew that this construction site was continually growing in height. It even seemed to me that there were cranes and scaffoldings, or perhaps they were rising parts of buildings. This object of gold, light, and radiant beauty was worked on incessantly and with great intensity.

Far away, a giant dome rose strikingly above the building site. It must have been extremely big. Jesus asked me, "What is that?" but I could not recognize what it was. Then I said to myself that it must be the throne room of God. I was surprised at first, but in a fraction of a second it seemed completely logical to me. I knew that the throne room of God constituted the center of the heavenly Jerusalem. Of course! What else could it be? Right at the central point of the heavenly Jerusalem is the throne room, the place of His presence.

"And the name of the city from that time on will be: THE LORD IS THERE [Jehovah Shammah]**" (see Ezekiel 48:35).**

I was impressed and understood the merging of the two visions of the throne room and the heavenly Jerusalem even more clearly. Both were one, but I had seen them from two different angles so far. The throne room is the center of the city of God. I understood now that this was not a normal dome, but the top of the sphere-shaped room, already half surrounded by the construction of the heavenly Jerusalem. Soon, the whole "building" would surround it completely. Therefore, the site must have reached a little over half of its completion. Jesus said, "It is growing fast!"

I thought about the living stones forming the heavenly Jerusalem, the living building material of this spiritual city that will last for all eternity. The more people on earth that accept Jesus as Lord and Savior, the more the city will grow. At one point, the last living stone will be put in, and the construction will have reached its total perfection.

Then Jesus directed my attention toward the river of the Holy Spirit flowing out of the heavenly throne room in two directions, like a mighty beam. I could not see anything, although I had expected the stream to exit the zenith of the dome like a mighty gush.

Inside, I realized that I should not trust my earthly, three-dimensional thinking. Here, there was no above or below. The sphere-shaped room in the middle, and therefore also the exiting stream of the Holy Spirit, was situated perpendicularly to my position, to what I perceived as above and below. The stream flowed horizontally, not vertically through the site. I understood that the stream was already surrounded by the growing building and had been "integrated" into the construction fabric. Just like a huge canal, the stream therefore flowed right through the building structure.

I was confused by this and thought about it. But then, Jesus said, "Watch! I want to show you something else!"

Straight away, I found myself on the inside of the construction, where the glowing stream of the Holy Spirit was flowing. The picture reminded me in a striking way of pictures I had seen in children's Bibles, illustrating the heavenly Jerusalem, with a straightly running, broad river, bordered by trees and golden buildings behind.

In these pictures, the bed of the river was a straight line, looking therefore more like a canal. What I saw in my vision was amazingly similar, even though it was not just two-dimensional in width and length, but also with the dimension of height. The mighty beam of fire and light ran straight through the construction. It really was a stream, even though it cannot be compared with an earthly river flowing in a riverbed. It was a golden beam of light streaming through the city. The structure of the city itself surrounded the stream on all sides at approximately half a mile.

The picture reminded me more of an enormous tube leading to the central point of the city, enclosed by the glorious, golden, radiating, complex parts of the building construction. It was like a magnificent, unswerving, three-dimensional avenue all around the river, with a diameter, in human terms, of approximately two kilometers. All in all, it did not appear plain or simply structured, but was made in a way that reminded me of the façades of an extremely beautiful, elegant promenade. There were many individual building parts, forming this amazing ensemble. Everywhere inside this "tube"—floating in mid-air like in the heavenly throne room—were countless people who were obviously ambling or strolling along. I also saw a great number of trees, however, without paying much attention to them in detail.

"There is a river whose streams make glad the city of God, the holy place where the Most High dwells. God is within her" (Psalm 46:4-5).

The effect which this enormous tube of hundreds of kilometers in length, in which there was no up and down, had on me is indescribable. The words that could describe it the best would be light, gold, and glory. And it reminded me of a street—an ineffably sublime, noble, dead-straight avenue.

"Then the angel showed me the river of the water of life, as clear as crystal, flowing from the throne of God and of the Lamb down the middle of the great street of the city. On each side of the river stood the tree of life" (see Revelation 22:1-2).

CHAPTER 59

A Building in Zion

It was shortly after midnight when I noticed that I was in the heavenly Jerusalem, in the magnificent avenue inside the huge tube. The river of the Spirit flowed freely through this impressive scenery, which must have been hundreds of kilometers long. Everything was shining in bright gold and seemed to glow from the inside out. In this picture of gold and light, I recognized structures which reminded me very much of earthly buildings, balconies, porticos, windows, and such. But at the same time it was different, more like light, and built of an unearthly substance.

In the street, I saw people everywhere, mostly strolling around in groups or gathered together in conversation. It did indeed remind me of a broad, earthly avenue, surrounded three-dimensionally by beautiful buildings. In the middle flowed the mighty stream.

Together with Jesus, we joined a group of people who immediately knelt before Him. He touched them gently on the head or caressed their cheek, telling them to get up. I had the impression of witnessing a greeting ceremony, and at the same time a gesture full of goodness and kindness.

I felt the desire to take a closer look at one of the buildings in this street, and immediately Jesus moved with me at great speed over a long distance in the street. Then we stood in front of a mighty, high rising portal. It reminded me of a well-kept palace gate. It stood open, and we entered. Everything was bright and shining. Inside the gate, I saw a huge atrium with a big pond. A majestic fountain stood in the middle. All around the pond were many trees, with a great number of singing birds. Here and there were benches. I observed the ground, which showed a pattern and reminded me of a tiled or mosaic floor. It was colorful, but in the sense of differently colored light woven together.

In the water, which was so deep that I could not see how deep it really was, a great number of fish were swimming around. I looked up, but even though we were inside of the heavenly city, I could not make out the upper limit of the room. It seemed as if we were underneath a clear sky, rising far and wide above us.

This inner courtyard was surrounded by galleries and colonnades. I noticed many round arches. Immediately, we were inside one of the galleries, and I had the impression it was on the second floor. On one side was the inner courtyard, behind the round arches. On the other side was a wall with big doors, situated far apart from one another.

Together, we entered through one of the doors, which Jesus had opened, and reached a huge library. I recognized that, once again, all earthly proportions and dimensions were not sufficient to describe what I saw. The room was simply huge, so big that its proportions rather obviously did not fit with the gallery. It was obvious that earthly measures were not applicable.

This library reminded me of the heavenly treasure house that I had seen before on different occasions. Here also were galleries going all around the vast inner room. The room faded into light fog towards the back, and the end of the room was not visible. Without being able to discern anything in detail, I noticed that the library was bustling with activity.

Jesus closed the door without any further explanations and opened another one, which we reached at the same instant. This time I was looking into the room which I had named the "heavenly treasure house," and into which I had already entered many times before. The proportions were like in the room we looked at before.

I knew that there were many other rooms of the same kind and rooms where the treasures of the harvest of our lives were kept.

We were suddenly once again outside the heavenly Jerusalem looking at it from a great distance. I noticed that the construction work had progressed quite a bit since I last looked at it. The speed of the progress of the construction was impressive.

Jesus said, "She is growing very fast now toward completion, and it will speed up even more. It won't be long before the last stone is put into place. Then the heavenly *shofar* will resound, and all earthly activity will come to a halt. Real soon now! Very soon!"

"Rejoice greatly, Daughter Zion! Shout, Daughter Jerusalem! See, your king comes to you, righteous and victorious.... Then the Lord will appear over them; his arrow will flash like lightning. The Sovereign Lord will sound the trumpet; he will march in the storms of the south" (see Zechariah 9:9, 14).

CHAPTER 60

The City That Will Remain Forevermore

Jesus was with me and said, "Come!" He put His arm around my back, and I had the impression we were moving through space at great speed. First, it seemed to me that there was blackness all around, then it changed to become a deep red, and finally, I saw that we were right in front of a gigantic golden surface.

I recognized that it was the outer wall of the heavenly Jerusalem. The golden surface stretched as far as the eye could see, perfectly even in all directions. It was smooth and without any joints. We were standing directly in front, so I touched the wall by putting the palm of my hand against it. Once again, I felt that this structure was alive. It was not pulsating, like earthly beings whose hearts are beating and pumping blood through the arteries, but rather like a burning, a flickering, or an inner "being in motion." No change at all was perceptible on the outside. It reminded me of fire and embers. On earth, all this would have been built with inanimate materials, but in the heavenly world it was filled and flooded with life, which went beyond my comprehension but was totally real at the same time. I understood that this whole being, this object, this city, was filled with divine life for all eternity.

Jesus said, "Put your ear against it!" I did as He said and listened. I heard something like a gushing, humming, or flowing. Some sort of noise, in any case, that was caused by movement. It did sound a bit like the rushing of blood through the arteries—but at the same time it was totally different. I heard this blazing and soft sound, like a melody, the sound of music from afar.

Then suddenly, we were at a great distance, and I saw the city once again as this bright, glowing cube of light, with the numerous different surfaces and layers of light. Once again Jesus said, "It is growing fast. And the time will come when the last stone will be put into place, when it will be completed to perfection very soon!"

I knew that the erection of the foundation and the first stages of construction of this heavenly structure had taken a long time, according to our human understanding. It probably took centuries. Everything had been prepared precisely with heavenly perfection. Every stone was precious, intended from all eternity for exactly the place where it was put. Each stone was infinitely important, for without it this construction would not be perfect. The more the construction progressed, the more quickly the work went.

Jesus looked at me and said, "This city will remain for all eternity. I have given everything for it. It is the house of God. Those who are part of the living house of God will live forevermore!"

"Instead, they were longing for a better country—a heavenly one. Therefore God is not ashamed to be called their God, for he has prepared a city for them" (Hebrews 11:16).

"My Father's house has many rooms; if that were not so, would I have told you that I am going there to prepare a place for you?" (John 14:2)

I realized that all the people who were not part of this building, who were not living stones in this eternal structure of God, would remain outside. The Bible talks about the fact that outside there will be wailing and gnashing of teeth. "To be outside" does not mean to be physically outside of the city—so to speak, in the vicinity of it—but it means not to be a part of it, to not be built into it. Those who are not inside the heavenly Jerusalem are outside of the life that God has planned for us.

"There will be weeping there, and gnashing of teeth, when you see Abraham, Isaac and Jacob and all the prophets in the kingdom of God, but you yourselves thrown out" (Luke 13:28).

"Nothing impure will ever enter it, nor will anyone who does what is shameful or deceitful, but only those whose names are written in the Lamb's book of life" (Revelation 21:27).

CHAPTER 61

The Construction is Growing

There was complete silence. I felt Jesus next to me, and we talked for a while. He put His arm around me, and I saw one of the corners of the heavenly Jerusalem rising in front of us.

We moved along one of the edges. I became aware of the absolute hugeness of this object, floating freely in space. Suddenly, we were traveling at high speed away from it, until we reached a point from which we were able to see the whole of the structure.

"The city with foundations, whose architect and builder is God" (see Hebrews 11:10).

I looked at the area where the building work was being done. Once again, the work had progressed since I had looked at it the last time. This time, the overwhelmingly huge building site really looked like the "construction of a city." The outer walls had also become higher as the building progressed, and they were totally even, smooth, flat, and made of living gold. The unfathomable size of the city captured me.

Then Jesus said: "It is growing fast and becomes more and more glorious. I love it! The day will come when the last stone will be put in. This will be a day of rejoicing on which the glorious bride will have reached perfection. This will be the day of My return, the day on which the trumpet will sound. The heavenly Jerusalem is the center of all things. It is the throne of God and the people of the Lord, gathering around it. It is the glory of all eternity; it is marvelous. It won't be long now, and when the last stone will be put in, the sound of the trumpet will be heard and shake the foundations of the world. Do you see the construction? Blessed is he who has the privilege to take part in the building. Without all those who join in the building, without each individual building stone, it would not be perfect. But not one stone will be missing, and every builder will complete his work. Every day, it grows faster."

What an uplifting thought: this is the city that will remain in all eternity! A little later, Jesus talked to me about the topic of eternity. He said, "Eternity. Eternity is something completely different than just an endless succession of time. Eternity is not time. Time will cease; eternity will remain. Death will cease; life will remain. Suffering will cease; joy will remain. Eternity is different from what you can imagine. In the same way as you cannot picture timelessness, or dimensional limitlessness, you cannot picture eternity."

He continued, "There will not be one second of boredom, dullness, or regret in the heavenly world. Boredom is something that belongs to the fallen creation, just like pain, suffering, need, discontentment, and sin. In eternity, you will be sure: 'I am where I am supposed to be. I am at home.' Eternity is something that goes beyond your human understanding. Look forward to it! Nothing is more terrifying than to be eternally separated from Me, and nothing is more glorious and fulfilling than to be united with Me. I have put eternity in your heart—in the heart of every man. The enemy has destroyed this awareness in many people because they have devoted themselves to the wrong things and listened to the wrong voices. But a touch of My goodness can rekindle this desire. Eternity is something that I have prepared for My children."

"He has also set eternity in the human heart" (see Ecclesiastes 3:11).

CHAPTER 62

In the Stream of the Spirit

I was next to Jesus and once again saw in front of me, at great distance, the apparition of the heavenly city. As before, it was surrounded by those fascinating spheres and structures of light. This time I saw more clearly that it looked like a square building stone, made of bright shining gold, and floating freely in space. I could see that, from my viewpoint towards the left, there was still construction work going on.

Viewed from my position, the stream of the Holy Spirit was flowing out horizontally to the right and the left of the structure. It continued straight as far as my eyes could see, and it was as if this stream, like a straight line, was dividing the picture before me in two parts, a bit like a horizon.

Suddenly, we moved towards the stream and stood directly next to it in an instant. Once again, I was so close to it that I could touch it with my hand. And again, it was this burning, glowing, golden flowing fire, reminding me of lava, which flowed past me with great power and speed in the form of a clearly defined jet. On earth, one would have thought that it must flow through a glass tube, because the jet was so clear-cut. It flowed out of the throne of God with undiminished intensity. Jesus said to me, "Step into it!"

The stream "thundered" past me at great speed, and I was slightly confused. But then I boldly stepped into it, and to my great surprise, it flowed right through me. I was not carried away with it as I had expected, but initially I remained where I was. The stream flooded through me with great power and reminded me of the picture that I had at the beginning, when the water of the clear brook flowing out from the cross had been flooding through me, through my body, and through my whole being. This was a similar situation. Holiness, the Spirit of God, was flowing through me. I was reminded that streams of living waters were supposed to flow out from within us.[30] The mighty power of this flowing movement was clearly perceptible, it was like rain pelting through me.

"From Zion, perfect in beauty, God shines forth. Our God comes and will not be silent; a fire devours before him, and around him a tempest rages" (Psalm 50:2-3).

After some time, I realized that the stream was now carrying me with it, moving me at great speed to a certain spot. Soon afterwards, I found myself standing next to the stream again. Jesus was at my side. I could not see the heavenly Jerusalem anymore. I asked Jesus where I was, and to my surprise, He answered, "In Germany!"

I could see nothing except darkness and this streaming, mighty beam of fire that was right next to us. The words "holy glow, divine ember" came to my mind. Jesus spoke to me and said that I must go into this fiery stream, this Spirit, this river of God, if I wanted to bring about the things of God. Only if it was flowing through me would it accomplish that which Jesus wanted to do through me. I would not be doing things with my little strength, but this mighty, gigantic stream would flow through me and accomplish the things that no power of darkness and no demonic structure can come against.

The stream of God is flowing like a river of living fire. It flows out of all those who are willing to be used, to be cleansed, and to be made ready for that which God wants to do and will do. This stream of the Spirit will also flow through Germany, will flow through people who have been positioned, chosen, and made ready by God to change this nation.

---

30 John 7:37-39

The stream of the Spirit is not something that can be made, produced, manipulated, or artificially generated by human methods. As humans, we are the channels, but it is the stream, the holy fire of God, which will accomplish anything. Those who are driven by the Spirit of God, those are God's children.[31] He Himself will transport us to where He wants us to be, in order to flow through us towards this dying, suffering world. This fire will hit Europe, it will hit Germany, and it will tear down the strongholds of darkness in one instant and let the light shine.

31 Romans 8:14

CHAPTER 63

The White Cloud

I met Jesus and was full of joy. I danced all around Him and then took Him in my arms. At one point, I looked down and noticed that I was wearing armor once again. The sword was strapped to my side. Jesus told me that I was always wearing this armor, as well as the white robe that I was clothed with.

He took my hand, and together we started to run. First, I did not notice the environment around us, but then I saw that we were directly in front of a mighty, white wall of clouds. This wall reminded me of a cloud in the earthly sense—much more so than anything else I had seen so far. In their efforts to depict the heavenly reality, artists generally include clouds in their pictures, but during the whole of my journey, I had not consciously noticed any clouds so far. However, this was definitely a white wall of clouds. There was a slight movement, just like when the wind gently drives along the clouds in the sky we know on earth.

Jesus held my hand and we moved inside the wall of clouds. The cloud enveloped us and gave me feelings of holiness, purity, and clarity. After a few moments, I was overwhelmed by a feeling of sinfulness and inadequacy. I felt like Peter, who said, "Go away from me, Lord. I am a sinful man."[32] It was not a nice feeling. During all my experiences and impressions, I had never been so conscious of being part of a fallen creation as I was in this precise moment. My feeling was, "I am a man of unclean lips, and I live among a people of unclean lips."[33] At the same time I knew that I had unhindered access to the Father through

---

32 Luke 5:8
33 Isaiah 6:5

Jesus, and that all my sin had been forgiven. I paused and asked Him to cleanse me. He touched me and I felt as if I could breathe freely again.

"What is this?" I asked.

"This is the Shekinah glory, the immediate presence of the Father. Where Jehovah is, there is also the Shekinah glory; there He is Himself."

"That the God of our Lord Jesus Christ, the Father of glory, may give you the Spirit of wisdom and of revelation in the knowledge of him" (Ephesians 1:17 ESV).

CHAPTER 64

The Glory of God

I saw Jesus, and we embraced each other. After a while, I asked Him to show me something, and He replied that He wanted to teach me something about the glory.

He explained that glory is not comparable to anything known on earth, and that human beings were not able to imagine what it was like. The glory is the presence of God made manifest—His nearness, His closeness. It has nothing to do with a cloud or fog in the earthly sense, even though there is no better word to describe its appearance.

He invited me to look at the throne room, in which I immediately stood. I noticed that it was filled with the cloud-like substance of this glory. I had never noticed this beforehand. It was a totally new vision. It was like thick fog, nevertheless I was able to see through it unhindered. Toward the throne, the cloud became even thicker, more "solid," white and radiant.

Jesus told me that this vision of the glory was the way the Father wanted to show and reveal Himself to me, and that it was the way He showed Himself to millions of other people. I asked myself if the beings in the heavenly throne room could see the glory of the Father also "only" in this way, but I received the answer that I could not perceive with my earthly eyes the things these beings were seeing. I knew that in Scripture, people had often seen God in the appearance of a human being. But God is not a person in the human sense, and any appearance of Him is just one single facet at a time—one out of myriads of facets.

Then Jesus taught me more. When Adam was hiding in the Garden of Eden, he did this because of the presence of God, because of the cloud of purity, of holiness, and clarity. He had sinned and knew that it would be terrifying to come into the immediate glory of almighty God. Therefore, he hid. This fleeing and hiding is the characteristic of fallen mankind. Man fears the presence of God, and he fears the eternal light and seeks the darkness.

Then Jesus spoke about the people who will be lost forever. They are people who will fear the light for all eternity and remain in the darkness. Just like heaven, eternal damnation and hell are things that go beyond our human understanding. Hell is remoteness from God, the absence of everything that is God, that which is beautiful and worth living for. Several Christians have received revelations about hell, about eternal damnation, but each of these revelations were only single facets. Some saw the lake of fire—it is real and one of the facets of the eternal separation from God. In the same way that we, as human beings, cannot imagine life in the eternal presence of God, we cannot imagine either the eternal separation from God. Human existence will not cease; all human beings will exist forever, either united with God or separated from God. Either they will live with the eternal knowledge, "I have come home," or with the eternal pain, "I am in the wrong place."

After that, the Lord spoke to me once again about the nature of born-again people, of the children of God. Each Christian is a temple of God, a temple of the Spirit and therefore also a representation of the heavenly reality.

"God's temple is sacred, and you together are that temple" (see 1 Corinthians 3:17).

God has made His dwelling in the inner man. He is present in it and wants to fill this spiritual temple with His glory and penetrate it with holiness, clarity, and purity. When someone is born again, He is directly linked to what is going on in the heavenly reality. He is put into the heavenly realm, blessed with every spiritual blessing in the heavenly places and directly connected with the heavenly reality.

"He has blessed us in the heavenly realms with every spiritual blessing in Christ" (see Ephesians 1:3).

"And God raised us up with Christ and seated us with him in the heavenly realms in Christ Jesus" (see Ephesians 2:4-6).

The Spirit dwelling in the born-again person is the same Spirit that flows out of the heavenly throne room. He wants to flow through us and through millions of His other children to do the works of God in this world. The stream of the Spirit wants to flow through our arms and hands to bring true life to this fallen creation, given over to death. Each Christian is a source of the Spirit, and in each Christian God's glory dwells in a secret place. Our mouths must be the mouth of Jesus, our eyes must be the eyes of Jesus, and our hands must be the hands of Jesus through which heavenly blessings will be released.

CHAPTER 65

The Glory of the Lord Will Fill the Earth

I noticed that I was once again with Jesus, standing in front of the cloud of glory. He took my hand, and we moved into the radiant whiteness. After a short while, I saw that we had reached the place with the fiery coals.

He kept holding my hand, looked at me, and said: "This is the origin of all existence, the place where the Spirit of God is brooding, right in the center of God's glory. The Father is here, the Spirit takes its origin here, and I, the Son, am here too. We have completely surrendered Ourselves to the people on whom the divine favor rests. The Father has created man and breathed His life into him. I have given My life for him. The Holy Spirit has been sent to the children on whom His favor rests and is at their disposal. The Father, the Son, and the Spirit have given Themselves freely. This is in all eternity the greatest of mysteries; this is why man has been created in the image of God. We have given ourselves to those who will give themselves to us."

"The mystery that has been kept hidden for ages and generations, but is now disclosed to the Lord's people.... Christ in you, the hope of glory" (see Colossians 1:26-27).

Straight after this, I saw the heavenly throne room. The golden throne itself was not visible anymore; it was surrounded by the cloud of the glory of the Lord, enveloping it completely like a very thick, white, radiating substance. This whiteness was very bright and shining, but it was more than that. On the inside, it glistened and shimmered. It was glowing, and it was as if small flashes of lightning were sparkling inside. Sometimes there appeared shadows of colorful refractions of light, like the color spectrum of a rainbow. The whole of the cloud of glory was alive and pulsating.

"Like the appearance of a rainbow in the clouds on a rainy day, so was the radiance around him. This was the appearance of the likeness of the glory of the Lord" (Ezekiel 1:28).

Soon after this, we were once again in front of the mighty white wall of clouds. I asked Jesus how big this cloud was, and He answered that it had no end, and that the glory of God was immeasurable. We moved inside the cloud of glory, and after a few moments, I felt as if I was bursting with joy. I frolicked around, did somersaults, scampered about, and twirled around. This verse came to my mind:

"You will fill me with joy in your presence" (see Psalm 16:11).

Suddenly, I saw the heavenly Jerusalem from the outside, like a golden object of light in front of me. I was able to oversee the entire structure and noticed something that I had never observed before. The entire structure was embedded in this cloud of glory; the entire object was enveloped in it. The presence of God completely penetrated everything.

"For the Lord will rebuild Zion and appear in his glory" (Psalm 102:16).

Just an instant later, I was at an even greater distance and saw the heavenly Jerusalem, with the surrounding surfaces and spheres of light. I noticed that everything was completely enwrapped by this white cloud of the glory of God.

Then, I found myself even further away so that the heavenly Jerusalem was like a small star sparkling on the horizon. Everything was still shrouded in this white presence of God.

At that moment, the Lord spoke to me that the glory of the Lord will at one time cover the whole earth—all-encompassing and immeasurably—just like "the blue of the firmament encompasses the earth." I heard Him say, "The earth is too small to not be completely engulfed by the presence of God."

"For the earth will be filled with the knowledge of the glory of the Lord as the waters cover the sea" (Habakkuk 2:14).

"For the earth will be filled with the knowledge of the Lord as the waters cover the sea" (see Isaiah 11:9).

He continued by saying, "My Shekinah glory is My visible presence on earth—visible in the burning bush, visible in the pillar of cloud and of fire, visible as I filled the tabernacle and the temple, and visible as I overshadowed Jesus in His mortal body. It was visible again and again to My children throughout history. My presence—perceived as fog, as light, as blessing, as a golden shimmer, as beams of light, as a glow—is not tangible, not palpable, and not describable. But it is unforgettable, healing, and the greatest blessing for every person who encounters it. My glory will engulf the whole earth, and it will touch each person in their innermost being. I will show My glory to everyone. Those who hate Me and love the darkness will be greatly distressed and frightened. Those who know Me and love Me with all their heart will experience the greatest joy."

"Be exalted, O God, above the heavens! Let your glory be over all the earth!" (Psalm 108:5)

"Blessed be his glorious name forever; may the whole earth be filled with his glory! Amen and Amen!" (Psalm 72:19)

"Your kingdom come, your will be done, on earth as it is in heaven" (Matthew 6:10).

Martin, it will be very soon that My glory will engulf the whole earth and fill the entire globe. Heaven will touch earth and penetrate it in a way that no man can imagine. Each person must choose between light and darkness, each one must decide for himself. My kingdom is coming. It will fill the earth. Something unimaginable, something new will come for My children, for the stones of the living Jerusalem, for My bride.

Life begins. Yes, true life begins.

Love and joy—for all eternity!

Tell My children I have more for them—more than they can conceive or imagine! I have given everything for them so that they may be able to receive everything."

"'What no eye has seen, what no ear has heard, and what no human mind has conceived'— the things God has prepared for those who love him" (see 1 Corinthians 2:9).

A while after finishing work on this manuscript, I experienced a profound vision which I want to share in this second edition.

Once again, I find myself together with Jesus before the clouds of glory. They tower above us like a wall, thousands of kilometers high. We're floating in space before them. Then, Jesus asks me to go into the clouds. I grasp His hand, and together we move again into the white-gold substance. It surrounds us immediately, and I notice once again how it doesn't just surround me, but also presses into and flows through me. I move through it, and at the same time, it moves through me. The clouds envelop me so gently. It feels like a delicate, incredibly thin film of oil, pleasant and very soft.

Jesus urges me to consider the glory more closely. The substance is luminous, bright, glowing, thick, and white, but sparkling and in motion within. Suddenly, it reminds me of lava, and instantly I understand that this manifestation of the glory shows the same substance as the river of the Spirit—only much lighter, less compact. It's almost like the different states of matter. The river acts like a fluid, the cloud like a gas, and the blazing, glowing, pulsing that lives within is in both. The manifest presence of God!

Only two days later, I find myself together with Jesus at the same place before the gigantic wall of cloud.

Suddenly, a thought comes to me. We find ourselves floating in space in front of this glory—what is happening behind us? Without thinking, I spin around, and to my surprise, I notice that I can see the earth. The picture is like a photo of the earth taken from space. I have a complete overview of it, and see it as a blue-white ball, one half basking in the bright light of the sun, and the other half shrouded in night.

Compared to the immeasurably huge cloud wall of glory, it seems surprisingly small and reminiscent of a little, colorful glass marble in front of an enormous, white-painted wall. I know if the glory were to move, it would completely envelop the earth in a split second. The glory of the Lord need not take the "trouble" to create space for itself on the earth, to be more present there, to permeate it. No, the earth simply sinks into the glory of God like a pebble that one throws into an ocean.

Nothing on earth can resist this glory in any way.

"And blessed be his glorious name for ever: and let the whole earth be filled with his glory; Amen, and Amen" (Psalm 72:19).

PART III

Your Personal Discovery Journey

If you belong to the kind of people who long to look into the heavenly reality, and if you want to start out on your personal journey of discovering the dimensions of heaven, then I would like to give you some tips that may help you along the way.

First, it is important that the spiritual vision is not something that happens automatically, something that takes hold of you, something that you cannot control, or which even takes complete control of you. Spiritual vision has its origin in a living, undisturbed relationship to your heavenly Father—Yahweh; to your Lord and Savior Jesus Christ—Yeshua; and to your advocate, counselor, and comforter, the Holy Ghost—the Ruach ha Kodesh.

CHAPTER 66

Surrender and New Birth

Here is the foundation: without being born again, you do not have access to heaven, neither now nor in eternity. That is why your conversion, surrendering your life to Jesus, and your new birth are essential.

In case you have not yet taken the step of personally surrendering your life to God, or if you want to do it consciously one more time, I advise you strongly to turn to Him in prayer with a sincere heart and pray the following prayer out loud. Not just as a formula, but as the starting point of your communication and relationship with God. Once you have said this prayer, continue talking to God and tell Him in your own words, honestly and without being "religious," what is on your heart.

Dear heavenly Father,

I give my life to You. I acknowledge that I am a sinner who has no means of my own to stand before You justified.

But through Jesus Christ, You have made a way for me to come to You unhindered. I now acknowledge and accept that You have done this for me. I acknowledge that Jesus lives for me and that He died and rose again for me. I acknowledge the sacrificial death of Jesus on the cross in my place. I now willingly claim this for myself.

Lord, I repent of the things that I have done wrong, knowingly or unknowingly. I ask You to lead me into the process of purification, sanctification, and growth. I want to live a different life. I want to live a life that is pleasing to You. Please let me grow and become spiritually mature. I accept all that Jesus has done for me. I accept Him as Lord, Savior, and Redeemer. Amen.

It is only through your honest, personal, conscious, and deliberate decision to accept Jesus Christ as Lord and Savior that you become a Christian. Through the work of the Holy Spirit, who takes up His dwelling in your spirit the moment you surrender your life to God, you will be born again. Like a baby, you will be born into the spiritual world.

"No one can see the kingdom of God unless he is born again" (see John 3:3).

CHAPTER 67

Lifestyle and Sanctification

Now begins the process of growing up, learning, and understanding. Now begins the lifelong process of sanctification through which you will become more and more mature in your relationship with God and come to know Him more and more.

During this process of growth, there will be numerous attacks from the enemy, temptations, and assaults on the mind, through which Satan and his followers will try to rob you, weaken you, stop you, and if possible, neutralize you. In overcoming these assaults, you will become stronger, gain more experience, and be more mature. God will never allow attacks against you that are more than you can cope with. The same way you must pass tests again and again in the natural at school, in professional training, at university, or at work, so it is in the spiritual. Unfortunately, many Christians stay stuck somewhere in this maturing process, and never enter the complete maturity God has planned for them.

For instance, it is a sign of immaturity that some Christians think they can live in a way that is against the commands and ordinances of God, since they are "under grace." They completely block out the importance of a godly lifestyle. In the same way, an exaggerated, pharisaical, legalistic attitude can be a sign of immaturity. Even holding on to old hurts, unforgiveness, living in conscious sin, dependence on other people, etc. are an indication that the person is immature. What is so good about the spiritual life is the fact that you can always turn to the Lord, confess the problem, and make a new start with Him. There is no problem that you cannot overcome with God's help. God has not meant you to remain in a state of immaturity. The Holy Spirit living in you only waits for occasions to minister to you, to lift you up, and help you on your way.

Practically speaking, sanctification means do not watch movies when you know that they are not good for you and will not be beneficial to you in your walk with God, even if other Christians are perhaps the ones tempting you to do it. Most movies are a considerable blockage to your ability to see spiritually. This is also valid for newscasts and similar programs. It is equally important what kind of books and magazines you are feeding your inner man, and music you are listening to. Does it glorify God, does it edify your spiritual man, or does it hinder you? The simplest would be to ask the Holy Spirit to show you clearly what is good and beneficial for you and what is not.

The Bible provides a very useful list showing which criteria the things that you occupy yourself with must meet:

"Finally, brothers, whatever is true, whatever is noble, whatever is right, whatever is pure, whatever is lovely, whatever is admirable if anything is excellent or praiseworthy think about such things" (Philippians 4:8).

In order to get to know God, you need to spend a lot of time in intimate fellowship with Him. Reading the Bible is vital. Nothing else is more reliable and clearer to reveal God and the supernatural reality to you. So, studying the Scriptures yourself is an absolute necessity. That which you fill yourself with is what will be inside of you. If you fill yourself with the things of the world, then they will determine your thinking. If you fill yourself with the truth of God, it will influence your thinking and your vision. So, I repeat what I have already said in the first part of this book, the Bible tells you this:

"Since, then, you have been raised with Christ, set your hearts on things above, where Christ is seated at the right hand of God. Set your minds on things above, not on earthly things" (Colossians 3:1-2).

Your prayer life, the times you spend worshiping God, expressing your love towards Him, thanking Him for everything He has done for you, spending time with Him and bringing your requests before Him, are very important. When you become more mature, you will discover that prayer is not a monologue that you recite before God, but a real dialogue. The Holy Spirit dwelling in you wants to communicate with you, always speaking to you as a counselor and comforter and having you listening to Him. Most of the time, this happens in a much less spectacular manner than many people imagine. It is Him speaking into your spirit, into your heart—a communication Spirit to spirit.

Quite a few Christians mistake this speaking of the Holy Spirit for their conscience. It is the gentle voice in you that reminds you, for instance, to pray for a certain person, to call someone and to ask for forgiveness, to visit someone who is sick, to switch off the TV and listen to good worship music instead, to put a certain matter right, to donate a certain amount, etc. Often, Christians brush this inner impression to one side and say to themselves, "I'll do it later." But in the end, they never do it. The more often you ignore this voice, the more difficult it will be for you to hear it. But the more often you do what it says, the easier it will be for you to hear it. It is essential for your spiritual growth to make room for the directions of the Holy Spirit and to obey them.

CHAPTER 68

The Baptism of the Holy Spirit

Any resistance against the Holy Spirit and His working in you, each disregard toward His person, will keep you in a state of spiritual immaturity. That is why a good part of the propaganda of the devil is directed against the person and the work of the Holy Spirit.

One big barrier can be fear of what could happen if you open yourself without reserve to the Holy Spirit. Fear is the opposite of faith. If that is your case, you should go to God and tell Him freely what you are afraid of, what reservations you have, and ask Him to reveal the truth to you. Check if it may be necessary to repent of your wrong way of seeing things.

I am personally convinced that the filling with the Holy Spirit—the baptism of the Holy Spirit—is the most important key to be able to see into the spiritual dimension. Our conversion is not the same as the baptism in the Holy Spirit. A personal Pentecost was necessary for the disciples and the first Christians, and so it is for us today. The baptism of the Holy Spirit is a sort of deeper conversion, reaching a deeper level in our relationship with God. Many people are Christians for several years before they consciously reach out to be personally filled with the Holy Spirit. And for that, you need trust, openness, and willingness.

Being filled with the Holy Spirit does not happen automatically, in some sort of mystical way, but it happens when you invite the Holy Spirit sincerely and with an open heart to come and fill you completely and to extend the lordship of God in your life. In the New Testament, the speaking in tongues, the supernatural ability to speak in an unknown language, was generally the sign for having experienced a personal Pentecost. Speaking in tongues is something that "launches" you into a new level in your spiritual life because you allow the Holy Spirit to speak out spiritual truths with your voice, things that are not influenced by your fallen earthly mind and your thinking infiltrated by the enemy. You are praying the secrets of God.

"For anyone who speaks in a tongue does not speak to men but to God. Indeed, no-one understands him; he utters mysteries with his spirit.... He who speaks in a tongue edifies himself,... I would like every one of you to speak in tongues" (see 1 Corinthians 14:2-5).

Extensive, prolonged speaking in tongues—for instance during our daily work, while driving the car, going for a walk, taking a shower, etc.—will help you make a big step towards a better understanding of the spiritual reality around you.

If you have not yet personally experienced the filling with the Holy Spirit, I recommend that you say a prayer like the following out loud and then continue praying. Allow the Holy Spirit to flow through you, to use your voice, to take away all fear and doubt, to engulf you in His Shalom peace and to take you into what He has prepared for you.

My tip: Keep at it, do not give up. Don't be discouraged if it sounds funny. When a baby learns how to speak, it won't speak in full sentences straight away either. Many people have made the experience that a relaxed atmosphere is helpful, to be alone and without any pressure or constraint, for example while taking a bath or when lying in bed at night.

Dear heavenly Father,

I ask You to fill me with your Holy Spirit, to give me the baptism of the Holy Spirit that Jesus promised in John 14:16-19 and in Acts 1:4-8, and that the first disciples experienced on the day of Pentecost, as well as millions of Christians have experienced it since.

I allow the Holy Spirit to flow out from me, as the Scriptures say, and to use my voice to do that. Let the fruit of the Spirit grow in me and shape my life more and more. Use my speech to glorify You.

Take all my life; I surrender the lordship of my life to You.

Amen.

CHAPTER 69

Spiritual Sight

In order to be able to see the spiritual world, you must first desire it. As I already said, it does not happen automatically. You must ask God again and again to open your eyes of the Spirit and to show you your personal access point. As for me, I had prayed the following for many years: "Open my eyes, Lord. I want to see Your glory," and "Let me see Your face."

The perception of the spiritual reality around you is under attack, which is why it is something that does not simply fall into our laps. You must press in with perseverance and determination, always keep going, and never give up. Many people who are used by God in a supernatural way have paid a personal price, whatever it may have been. People who move forward spiritually often experience incomprehension, rejection, mockery, accusations, and reproaches.

The way people perceive the spiritual reality can vary a lot. Some Christians, for instance, mainly have dreams. Others can see angels and perhaps even demons. Still others experience physical manifestations when they see something. Some have visions with open eyes and audibly hear God's voice. Others have radiant faces after they have experienced something supernatural. Some have visions in their everyday life, whereas others experience these things mainly during times of prayer and fasting and so forth. What the Lord has for you He will have for nobody else in the exact same way.

Say a prayer like the following and make it the call of your heart. I am sure that the Lord is already waiting for it and rejoicing that you come to Him with this request.

Dear heavenly Father,

Open my spiritual eyes and let me see. I want to see You, Your glory, and all that You have prepared for Your children in the heavenly places, the inheritance of the saints in the light. Grant me a glimpse into the heavenly dimension, into the spiritual reality that surrounds me, so that I can perceive it with open eyes. Open my understanding and my spiritual perception. Take me on my personal journey of discovering heaven.

Take everything that hinders me and remove any spiritual barrier or veil. I give You my lack of faith, my faintheartedness, my self-centeredness, my looking at the things of this world. Help me develop faith, trust, and a confident assurance, as well as a deep and heart-felt love relationship with You, out of which can come true spiritual discernment. Open my eyes, Lord! Amen.

Growing and moving forward spiritually is a lifelong process. There will never come a point where you have reached all that God has prepared for you. You can always, constantly, each day of your life, until the Lord will call you to leave this earth, become more mature, grow, and press into a greater spiritual authority and power. It does not matter how old you are and how far you have already come in your life of faith. You must know this: **God still has more for you!**

Made in the USA
Columbia, SC
20 February 2024